Fur War

THE POLITICAL, ECONOMIC, CULTURAL AND ECOLOGICAL IMPACTS OF THE WESTERN FUR TRADE 1765–1840

April 1792   Opitsaht is bombarded and burned by Captain Robert Gray destroying 200 long houses, boats, food and equipment representing thousands of hours of work.

DAVID A. BAINBRIDGE

Layout and text design: David A. Bainbridge and AuthorImprints
Illustration credits at back of book
Cover image by Mark Myers

*Rio Redondo Press Mission: Advancing sustainability accounting
and reporting, increasing sustainable management of resources
and people, and protecting future generations.*

Manufactured in the United States of America First Edition ©2020

Contents

The Challenge of History

Working on the history of the fur trade in the West is as challenging as running treacherous rapids with a fully loaded canoe. It is not for the faint-hearted.

Events are rarely well defined or described the same way by different participants, biographers and historians. A researcher often feels that he has fallen into the famous Japanese film, *Rashomôn*,[1] where a violent event of feudal times is revealed through the eyes of the different participants.

Dates are often precise but may disagree by days, years, or decades. Names are very confusing as writers relied on phonetic spelling, alternative translations from foreign languages, conversations (that may have involved considerable use of alcohol); and later, dim memories of events recalled from decades earlier. Most fur trade accounts substituted simpler names for natives and many native workers ended up with four or more. Tribal names were misunderstood, mangled and confused.

The Flatheads[2] for example, have normal head shapes, and the reason for this name is unknown, perhaps related to a hand sign. European and American men favored giving their first male child the same name and the *Jr.* or *Sr.* is rarely noted. Native people often passed the name from father to son when the father retired. Forts and outposts often had the same name or multiple names even at the same time. There were, for example, at least five Fort Williamses.

Writing in their journals at the time, the participants edited out their own worst behavior and practices. The rapes, killings, abuse and mistreatment of, and by, their employees and natives were glossed over. Slaves were taken, sold, and abused but rarely mentioned. Massacres and acts of random violence are often downplayed or left out of accounts.

I have done my best to report the most likely version of events. As a scientist I was surprised by the number of errors I have seen in other books, websites, and articles. These are often propagated across the web. In addition, there are exaggerations and embellishments made by those writing up the stories told by others in an effort to make books more salable.[3] Several recent books have added excellent information from newly-found, or translated, original sources. The web has made original information available in ways that would have astonished a historian working just a few years ago.

For example, it is a delight to be able to search the church records of early New Orleans with just a few clicks of the mouse to find marriage information.

Prelude

efore the explorers and fur traders arrived, hundreds of thousands of people lived in the area that would be affected. Some of the highest population densities in North America were found along the coast, just as they are today. In some areas, villages reached more than 1,500 residents. Hundreds of tribes and tribelets thrived along the coast, inlets, and rivers. Life was good for most of these people in these resource-rich ecosystems.

Families could watch their children grow and have children of their own with little expectation of change. Some tribes were allies, others enemies, but most lived stable lives with little strife. Trading

Teamwork helped harvest rich marine resources.

took place across hundreds, and in some cases thousands, of miles. Some tribes relied heavily on slaves and slave raiding affected some of the weaker tribes.

Nature could still spring surprises and upset life. The tectonic plates that meet on the Fur Coast could (and will again) trigger massive earthquakes and tsunamis. The magnitude 9 quake on January 26, 1700 caused massive damage and loss of life as a tsunami more than 50 feet high hit many areas. The waves generated by this quake were so large that they caused considerable damage in Japan. Severe storms could lead to losses of hunters and traders at sea, and heavy rains could trigger landslides, like the massive Ozette slide[4] 300 years ago.

Welcome strangers!

The first visitors to the coast were almost invariably treated well by native people who were curious about these new arrivals. This would not last....

A Cautionary Note on Names and Terminology:

Word choices can be very challenging in discussing cultural history. Most people now consider "First Nations" to be a better term than "Indian tribe", avoiding Columbus's error. A First Nation may include many bands, tribes, tribelets or villages. Languages can be quite complex with considerable variation even within a First Nation. The Haida language was once spoken in more than 30 different dialects, but today only three remain. Much has been lost as the richness within these languages diminished.

Indian, native, aborigine, tribe, and other terms may have different but specific meanings in legislation and legal matters in

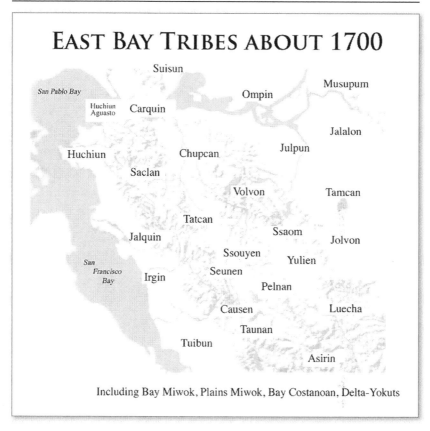

East Bay Tribes about 1700

Suisun

Musupum

San Pablo Bay

Ompin

Huchiun Aguasto

Carquin

Jalalon

Huchiun

Chupcan

Julpun

Saclan

Volvon

Tamcan

Tatcan

Ssaom

Jalquin

Jolvon

Ssouyen

Yulien

San Francisco Bay

Seunen

Irgin

Pelnan

Causen

Luecha

Taunan

Tuibun

Asirin

Including Bay Miwok, Plains Miwok, Bay Costanoan, Delta-Yokuts

Canada, the U.S., and Mexico. Names and boundaries are problematic at best, and even in the well-studied areas they are often unknowable. (In some cases, only the name is known and nothing else.) Tribes and tribelets often combined after severe population and property losses. In 1857 the U.S. government created the Grand Ronde Reservation as a place for the survivors of 26 tribes and bands in the Northwest.

First Nations people today often choose to use different names than anthropologists or federal bureaucrats. Many early tribal names were determined by European invaders. Some are still used. but many First Nations have reclaimed their original names. The Kumeyaay have done an excellent job of highlighting books that more accurately portray their history (www.kumeyaay.info/books/).

For many tribes little more than the name is known. California, for example, had more than 109 languages spoken. See the map on the previous page for the tribal names we know east of San Francisco Bay. Details of their life before the invasion are often unknown. Many disappeared with hardly a trace.

Translations and transliterations between Russian, Spanish, French, American, native languages, and English are often confusing. Native names were heard quite differently by the visitors from foreign lands. I have tended to use Russian names and spellings for lesser-known characters but the more accepted English for the better known.

CHAPTER 1

Geopolitics of the Fur Trade in the West

The fur trade played a key role in the development and ultimate ownership of lands and resources on the West Coast of North America. The struggle played out far from the capitals of power and shifted over time as rulers, governments, tribes, companies and individuals struggled to get rich or merely to survive. The players in this complex conflict included Russia, Great Britain, America, France, Spain, Mexico, Hawaii, and the many First Nations whose lands it had been. At times the fur trade was incredibly profitable and helped make some men and women very rich. The economic returns and taxes also helped support governments. But like most "gold rushes" it more often led to suffering, abuse, death, and despair for the sailors, trappers, and fur traders involved. Like gold rushes elsewhere, the most profitable period was very short.

The impact was terrible for the many First Nations whose lands were invaded (more in Chapter 3). Abuse and conflicts led to resistance and warfare that in some cases decimated local communities.

Many native villages had hundreds of residents, more than all the Russians on the entire coast and the white population of the Willamette Valley in 1840.

More often it was not deliberate genocide because the natives were needed to collect the furs, but they had little or no resistance to introduced diseases. Beginning at first contact with explorers, a series of epidemics of small pox, malaria, influenza, syphilis and other diseases[5] swept through the region; these often killed 50–90% of the people in tribal groups. The intermittent fever (malaria) of the 1830s was introduced by a fur-trading vessel and spread by the Hudson's Bay Company trappers. It was particularly destructive in Oregon and California and would remain to torment and kill many gold seekers in California after 1849. The death of so many native people led to social disruption in even the strongest tribal groups. Many tribes and tribelets were gone before they were noted in a journal or placed on a map. While it was not intentional genocide, the results were the same, mirroring the Jewish holocaust or the Palestinian *Nakba*.[6] The virtual disappearance of many tribes made future settlement by Europeans and Americans much easier from Baja California to Alaska.

The native men were often forced by the Russians to hunt far from home, leaving the women, children and elders to survive very trying circumstances. The men might be gone for years, dropped off a ship on some rocky island to hunt for furs and would survive as best they could. Native hunters working for the fur companies were often killed by natives in the regions where they were collecting furs. They were also at risk from the severe storms that often occurred. In some years, parties of more than 500 *baidarkas*[7] set out upon perilous journeys following the line of the coast for more than 1,000 miles. In one year a third of the fleet was lost on the way. Shelikhov and others also took the excellent fur suits from the natives and replaced them with Chinese cotton, ill-suited to wet and cold conditions. At Kukak, a village opposite Kodiak on the Alaska Peninsula, only 40 of 1,000 men remained in 1805. Over the preceding ten years the Russians had taken the rest of the men away to hunt sea otters with most never to return.

There was no one to stand up for native people until the Russian Orthodox Church arrived. In California the story was different and missionaries were more often a problem than a source of relief. The mission of San Diego de Alcalá was established in 1769, and the missionaries and soldiers so infuriated the Kumeyaay that they attacked and burned the mission in 1775.

Resistance continued, but the more effective weapons and soldiers of the Spanish led to more and more natives being held, often against their will, on the missions for labor and conversion. Too often the conversion was fatal.[8]

In this book I try to provide a new view of the fur trade on the West Coast exploring the cultural, political, and environmental consequences of the rush to collect furs. This new look is important because this period is so often neglected in history books. Programs and books about California history typically skip from the missions and *Californios* (Spanish and Mexican ranchers) to the Gold Rush.

The 75-year period from 1765–1840 covers the most critical period of the fur trade from the early days of sea otter slaughter in Alaska to their near total destruction by 1830. The beaver fell to the trappers next, and many other fur bearers were mercilessly hunted. By 1840 the beaver trade had also collapsed with the advent of the silk top hat. In the same year the first wagon reached Oregon. The Russian fur outpost at Fort Ross was sold to John Sutter in 1841. The exodus of the Hudson's Bay Company traders from Oregon continued with the creation of Fort Victoria on Vancouver Island in 1843 and the boundary settlement of 1846.

THE FUR TRADE COMPETITORS

The major players in the competition for furs were the Russians, English and Americans, with lesser but still important actions from Hawaii, Spain and Mexico. Many traders made bold and successful journeys and decisions, while others made terrible and costly blunders. Leadership problems in distant capitals played a major role in the final outcome. Over these years the Russians had four leaders, the Spanish five, British two, Americans eleven, Hawaii three, and in just 25 years, the Mexicans had more than thirty. The major fur trade contenders were also engaged in a series of shooting wars among themselves and with others in shifting alliances over this period.

Conflicts included the U.S. War of Independence, the Anglo-Dutch War, the Anglo-Spanish War, a series of costly Napoleonic wars, the Anglo-Russian war, the Spanish-Portuguese War, the War of the Oranges, the Haitian Revolution, War of 1812, three Russo-Turkish Wars, the Mexican War of Independence, the Portuguese Civil War, the Hawaiian Wars of Consolidation, a war between England and France, the Russian-Swedish War, and the First Opium War. These all diverted attention, resources, and people from the struggle for domination of the fur trade and the lands of the West Coast. At the same time the fur trade often added much needed money to the government coffers.

THE RUSSIANS

The development of the fur trade in the West began with adventurers from Russia after the sea otters of the western Pacific islands became scarce. In 1741 the Danish captain Vitus Bering and the German naturalist Georg Wilhelm Steller reached Alaska on the

Russian ship *St. Peter*. They later shipwrecked and Bering died, but the survivors lived on sea cow meat and other mammals and eventually made it back to Kamchatka with 900 sea otter furs. Their fortunes were made and the "soft gold rush" was on.

Russian adventurers, *promyshlenniki*, sailed in increasing numbers to the Aleutian Islands and later to the coast of Alaska.

Courageous crews on small Russian ships pursued the soft gold. The shitik was able to land on any beach.

From 1743 to the founding of the Russian-American Company in 1799, more than 150 private fur-trading and hunting voyages were made from Kamchatka and Okhotsk to North America. These hunting parties could be very profitable. In 1787, Erasim Gregorian Sin Izmailov returned to Kamchatka with furs worth 172,000 rubles. Although the market was almost entirely in China, Izmailov tried to throw the British off the trail by saying the otters were going to Japan. In total, the Russian privateers brought back furs worth more than eight million silver rubles (perhaps $2 billion in today's dollars).

The *promyshlenniki* fur traders typically operated small ships[9] with crews of 40–70, often with many Siberian or Kamchatka natives in the crew. The typical fur hunt lasted 2–6 years and required wintering over. The risks, costs and profits were shared in a variety of

ways. A typical cruise might offer a share to each Russian participant. The natives might get a half-share. The captain and navigator might get two shares or more.

Shelikhov and others also charged everyone for all the food they ate, the clothes they wore, and more. By the end of a cruise the low-level workers might owe as much or more than they earned.

Enterprising and often ruthless promyshlenniki came from Russia, Kamchatka and Siberia.

The *promyshlenniki* had not treated the natives of Kamchatka well and they treated the native Alaskans poorly.

Women and others were taken as hostages, workers, and sex partners. The local people bravely resisted the abuse of the Russians but faced insurmountable odds against guns, cannons, and ruthless

The first Russian settlement was at Iliuliuk, Unalaska.

traders. As conflicts with the native people intensified they killed more Russians, and then retaliatory massacres took place.

The first permanent Russian settlement was made in at Iliuliuk on the island of Unalaska on the north side of the Aleutians in 1768.[10] In 1784 the Shelikhovs set up the second permanent settlement at Three Saints Bay on Kodiak (Koniag) Island. Alexander A. Baranov moved the Kodiak Island settlement from Three Saints Bay to Pavlovsk after the earthquake and tsunami of 1786. In 1793, Baranov founded the port of Voskresensk in Chugach Bay, and then a settlement in Yakutat Bay in 1795. A network of trading posts eventually covered the area.

Natalia Shelikhov and others lobbied tirelessly and effectively in St. Petersburg and the Russian American Company (RAC) was chartered in 1799 with a monopoly on the fur harvest from Alaska. In return, the RAC would provide a better organized and financially stable company to protect Russian national interests, much like the role the Hudson's Bay Company played for England. Alexander Baranov became the manager of the RAC in 1799 and started the New Archangel (later Sitka) settlement on Sitka Sound. As activities moved south the RAC established Fort Ross on California's northern coast in 1812. In 1818, a new rule was put in place in an effort to reduce the abuse of natives and workers. This required the governor of the RAC to be a naval officer. This did improve management in some respects but diminished the innovation and enterprise of the original company employees.

The Russian fur trade began in the Aleutians and worked its way east, north to the Pribilofs, and south, through Alaska, the northwest coast, and far down the coast of Baja California. Land furs, including beaver and fox, were collected, but the sea otter was the primary target.

Much of the otter hunting was done by native people in specially constructed fur trade *baidarkas,* with fleets of many hundred hunters. This method was later adopted by the Americans, often in cooperation with their Russian rivals.

The Russian settlements were severely hampered by the distance from the sources of supply. The overland journey from St. Petersburg to Okhotsk was 5,000 rugged miles, and then supplies had to cross the treacherous waters of the Sea of Okhotsk and the Gulf of Alaska. The sea routes from the Russian port of Kronstadt were longer (16,000 miles) but less dangerous. Shipping by sea cost only one-third as much but took much longer. As a result, the Russian fur-trading posts were almost always short on supplies.

Despite efforts to suppress the trade with foreigners, many supplies and ships came from America and England. Sixty-one of the seventy-two ships that visited Russian America between 1787 and 1806 sailed from Boston. After the Imperial Russian government became alarmed by reports of American influence the tsar enacted an *Ukase* on September 4, 1821, prohibiting all foreign merchant ships from trading with Russian colonies. This was a catastrophic development and led to severe hardship in Alaska. As a result, it was

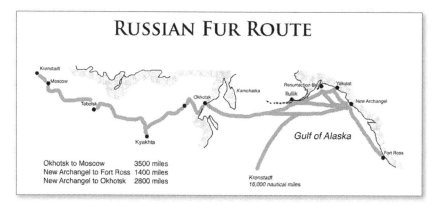

RUSSIAN FUR ROUTE

Kronstadt
Moscow
Tobolsk
Kyakhta
Okhotsk
Kamchatka
Illiulik
Resurrection Bay
Yakutat
New Archangel
Gulf of Alaska
Fort Ross

Okhotsk to Moscow   3500 miles
New Archangel to Fort Ross 1400 miles
New Archangel to Okhotsk   2800 miles

Kronstadt
16,000 nautical miles

New Archangel (now Sitka) settled in 1799, thrown out by Tlingit in 1802, retaken in 1804.

soon ignored and perhaps a million rubles in trade with foreigners was conducted from 1820–1825.

The low numbers of Russians in Alaska and along the coast to the south were a persistent problem. By 1817, some 450–500 *promyshlenniki,* a few Kamchatka natives and *kreols,*[11] and 26 sailors lived in 16 settlements stretching from the western end of the Aleutian Chain at Adak to Russian America's southeastern terminus at Fort Ross—this was fewer people than in a typical coastal tribal village before contact. Some authors suggest there were never more than a thousand Russians in all of Russian America—an area about as large as the Spanish territories stretching from Mexico to Peru. Efforts to recruit skilled settlers were rarely successful, although some Finnish, Baltic Germans, and European Russian workers were enticed to come to the North in later years. Efforts to send the mixed race *kreols* to Russia for advanced education and training met with limited success.

The Russian settlement at Fort Ross was started in 1812 to improve the supply situation. Agricultural production in California helped meet the need for food in the northern settlements. Fort Ross became a multi-ethnic community that functioned well and was fondly remembered by many of the Russians. The Russians there interacted well with local natives and American traders, but not so well with Spanish and then Mexican governments.

In 1824, the Russo-American Treaty released Russian claims on the Pacific northwest coast of North America, south of parallel 54°40'N, to the United States. They did however maintain Russian rights to trade south of that latitude. In 1822, the charter for the Russian-American Company permitted the Russians to conscript half of the adult native male population between the ages of 18–50 to work for up to three years hunting sea otters. This crippled the native hunters' ability to provide food for their families and to participate in child rearing.

Russia and England agreed on a follow-up to the Russo-American treaty that more clearly defined the boundaries between Russian America and British claims and possessions in the Pacific northwest of North America, again at parallel 54°40'N with associated rights and obligations concerning waters and ports in the region. The treaty, in establishing a vague division of coastal Russian interests and inland British interests northward from 56 degrees north, led to conflicting interpretations of the meaning of the treaty's wording which later resulted in the Alaska boundary dispute between the United States, Canada, and the British Empire.

The treaty also included the British right to navigate for both commerce in the region and access to rivers crossing the designated boundary. These rights were exercised by the Hudson's Bay Company in 1834 but opposed by the Russian-American Company

Fort Ross was founded in 1812. This multicultural Russian outpost north of San Francisco developed good relations with the local people.

with warships and a blockade. The *Dryad* affair led to a new Russia-HBC[12] agreement in 1839, with the RAC leasing the mainland portion of the region south of Cape Spencer to the HBC for the annual rent of 2,000 seasoned land otter skins. They also promised to supply Russian America with wheat, flour, salted meat, butter, and other supplies at a fixed price. The HBC waived its demand for payments for damages incurred during the *Dryad* affair.

The Russian fur trade declined steadily but they remained active. In 1842 for example, Lavrentiy Zagoskin led a two-year expedition that investigated the Yukon, Kuskokwim, and Innoko River drainages. This led to more beaver being taken from these northern rivers. Zagoskin's research would later prove useful in the Yukon Gold Rush in 1896.

Russian fur-hunting ships remained active far down the coast of Baja California through 1830. The *Baikal*, for example, was given permission to hunt from Mission San Luis Rey (San Diego County) to Todos Santos in 1826, collecting 468 otter furs in three months. A short-lived RAC fort and outposts were also established in Hawaii.

THE BRITISH

In 1776, Captain James Cook was provided with two ex-coal scows, *HMS Resolution,* and *HMS Discovery,* to continue exploration and survey work in the Pacific. Among the many men on the crew were a handful of Americans, including John Ledyard from Groton, Connecticut. On his third voyage, Cook sailed to the Northwest coast and in 1778 he reached Alaska. In May of that year they were surrounded by *baidarkas* at their anchorage in Snug Corner Cove on Prince William Sound. This area had not yet been traumatized by the *promyshlenniki* and Captain Charles Clerke noted, "...*they are a very happy race.*" The crew also picked up some sea otter pelts and fur clothing to help them stay warm aboard ship.

Captain Cook was killed in Hawaii in 1779 after a struggle over a small boat stolen from his ship. Lack of understanding and cultural awareness (and perhaps Cook's frustration after too many

The western world learned about the valuable furs from Cook's third voyage.

years at sea) led to the death of a native chief. This in turn led to the assault that killed Cook. *HMS Endeavor* later fired on the native village killing many Hawaiians. When Cook's ships reached Canton, China they sold their sea otter pelts for $100 each. Sailors made dramatic profits on the sea otter skins they had picked up and used as blankets on the ship. The price for a prime hide represented more than two years' wages (annual salary for a seaman in the Royal Navy was just £10, or about $44). A good pelt was worth the equivalent of about $2,000 in today's dollars (If we consider the value in relation to salary it would be closer to $20,000). The potential for enormous profit was clear.

The first trading vessel on the coast after the Russians was the British *Sea Otter* commanded by James Hanna in 1785. In a brief visit to the coast he obtained 560 pelts worth £7,000 in Canton. George Dixon and Nathaniel Portlock, also former members of Cook's crew, became partners in the King George's Sound Company (1785) to pursue the fur trade. They sailed from England (with permission) on the *King George* under Captain Portlock, and the *Queen Charlotte* under Captain Dixon. They spent 1786 and 1787 exploring and trading on the Northwest Coast where British ships from India were on the coast illegally. In 1787, Charles William Barkley on the *Imperial Eagle* sailed to the Northwest Coast from England via Hawaii under an Austrian flag. In 1787, the *Prince of Wales,* under Captain James Colnett, and the sloop *Princess Royal,* under Captain James Duncan, also made it to the coast.

John Meares resigned from the British navy to form a company to trade furs on the Northwest coast. His first trading voyage to Prince William's Sound, Alaska in 1786 was tragic and many sailors died from scurvy. He returned to Nootka Sound in 1788 with two ships under Portuguese flags. He bought[13] some land and built a temporary trading post where his men constructed the *North West America*, the first ship built on Canada's west coast. In 1789, Meares formed a new company with other British entrepreneurs and sent three ships to build a permanent trading post at Nootka and to trade widely on the Northwest Coast but found a Spanish naval force in place that quickly seized the British ships and crews.

The British traders worked the coast effectively but were hampered by the monopoly of the East India Company and South Sea Company in selling furs and other goods in Canton. These bureaucracies added many costly burdens in fees, graft, and time. The English ships were less efficient than the Americans, with larger crews and less skillful sailors.[14] The British crew and officers were typically salaried instead of holding shares like the Americans; this reduced hustle, increased cost, and reduced profits.

The English were more active in the inland fur trade at first, going after beaver from their eastern outposts. Explorers added new routes and improved communication overland to Montreal but the costs were high. Once British ships arrived on the coast regularly they offered a western outlet and profits increased.

This effort was part of a larger goal to develop and protect British interests against both the Russians and Americans. In a February

1822 letter from HBC's Governing Committee to George Simpson, they wrote, "*The Russians are endeavoring to set up claims in the North West Coast of America as low as Latitude 51°, and we think it desirable to extend our trading posts as far to the West and North from Fraser's River in Caledonia, as may be practicable, if there appears any reasonable prospect of doing so profitably.*" The British did eventually set up and manage a very effective group of trading posts for inland furs.

The American fur traders were also getting more active on land, following the ill-fated Astorians of 1811. In 1824, despite the joint occupation convention signed in 1818, both Britain and the United States were anxious for clarification of their claims to the region. The British wanted to maintain their claim south to the Columbia River and the Americans wanted to push the British back to the 49th parallel or further north. George Simpson directed HBC trapping parties to clear fur-bearing animals from the Snake River region to create a "fur desert" to dampen the American westward push. This HBC effort was attacked in 1837 in Congressional testimony in Washington, D.C. by William Slocum.

This helped fuel antagonism between the Americans and British in the Northwest. The fur desert was an example of international political efforts using the destruction of natural resources as a political weapon. This decision would affect the environment and the local inhabitants—first the natives, then British, and Americans for generations.

THE AMERICANS

When John Ledyard was a young man he dropped out of Dartmouth College, built a canoe, took it down the Connecticut River to the sea, signed on as a sailor, and kept traveling until his unfortunate death in Egypt in 1789. He was probably the first American to the fur coast, serving as corporal of marines on Cook's momentous third voyage. He learned the value of sea otter fur in Canton, and in 1783, after deserting from the British navy, he returned to Connecticut and published his journal about Cook's voyage. He included a note on the value of sea otters in China, *"It afterwords happened that skins which did not cost the purchaser sixpence sterling sold in China for 100 dollars. Neither did we purchase a quarter of the beaver and other furr skins we might have done, and most certainly should have done had we known of meeting the opportunity of disposing of them to such an astonishing profit."*

Ledyard clearly saw the future of the fur trade and tried very hard to kick-start it by proposing a three-way trade similar to what ultimately developed. He proposed a voyage around Cape Horn to Nootka to collect furs, then selling them at Macao (China), trading for Chinese goods and then ultimately returning to Boston via Capetown. He exhausted every avenue to raise funds in the U.S. and Europe to no avail. In Paris in 1784 he pitched his proposal to Thomas Jefferson, then the United States minister to France. Jefferson saw the potential value of the fur trade in the West and was then inspired to send Lewis and Clark across the country to the Pacific.

Although British members of Cook's expedition returned to the coast first, Boston ships were not far behind. In 1787, *Columbia Redivivia* under John Kendrick, and Robert Gray in *Lady Washington*, left Boston for the fur coast. They found that copper and firearms were the most desired trade goods on the coast and used them to amass a cargo of otter pelts. They traded, explored, spent much of the winter ashore and encountered other traders, including a British ship operating under a Portuguese flag. With a load of otter pelts, *Columbia* set off for China in July of 1789. When questioned by a Spanish vessel (remember, this was nominally land and water owned by Spain at the time) the Americans claimed they were merely "explorers."

Captain Gray stopped in Hawaii, re-provisioned, and then sailed to Canton where he sold 1,250 pelts for $21,400 (more than $600,000 in today's dollars). In Hawaii he met and became familiar with the native men, or *kanakas*, who would play an important role in the fur trade all along the west coast and far into the interior.

Almost half of the money he made was needed to refit[15] the ship for the voyage home. With a modest cargo of tea and other goods, the *Columbia* reached Boston in 1790, the first American ship to circumnavigate the world.

By the time the numbers were added up, the voyage had lost money, but Gray persuaded investors to finance another trip and he was back on the coast by 1792. In a confrontation with natives he used the ship's cannons to kill two of the tribal leaders. On this voyage, Gray wintered on the coast instead of going to Hawaii. His crew built a house, dubbed Fort Defiance in Clayoquot Sound. They also built the first American vessel on the northwest coast. Gray concentrated on the southern part of the northwest coast, including the large river that he "discovered" and named Columbia.

This trip and others were successful and soon many American ships were trading on the Golden Round from Boston to Hawaii, to the northwest coast and on to Canton, China, and then back to Boston. During the peak years (1790s–1810) the trade on the southern part of the northwest coast had so largely fallen into the hands of Boston traders that the Indians called all Americans "Boston men" to distinguish them from the British "King George's men." Nootka Sound was humorously referred to as a suburb of Boston. Trade increased rapidly along the coast wherever sea otters could be found.

The *Jefferson,* under Captain Josiah Roberts, found the trade so good that they exhausted all of their popular trade goods. They then traded all the less popular iron work, then *clamons* (elk armor) collected in trade further south, clothing made from sails, and finally, they stripped the ship of almost anything that could be spared, including the long boat, jolly boat, ship's crockery, and oil skins. The Yankee traders found the native people to be shrewd and aggressive bargainers and eventually learned of the extensive inter-tribal trade that had been carried out before the Europeans arrived.

From 1790–1810, as many as 100 American ships reached the northwest coast. They were unparalleled in their success because

In 1811 the Americans built Fort Astoria near the mouth of the Columbia River.

they had strong financial incentives, total flexibility, and efficient ships and sailors. Captains were often part owners. The most generous ship's owners split shares at 50% for the owner, 10% to the captain, 7% to supercargo (sales manager), and the rest was split among mates and crew. In some cases, the captain and officers were also allowed to do some trading of their own. Other captains only gained a share of 1–6% with the crew paid a flat rate and charged heavily for all supplies. Sometimes the shares applied only to the Canton sales; in other cases, for all sales, including the northwest coast, China, and Boston.

The most noteworthy captains, like William Sturgis, respected the native people and traded for years without incident. Others treated the natives like animals and stole furs, took women, held hostages for fur ransoms, shot people with no provocation, blasted and burned villages, and otherwise laid what would become fatal traps for future ships and crew.

The American ships covered the coast up to and past Russian holdings and far to the south. As the northern otter populations declined under enormous hunting pressure the otter hunt moved further south. In 1804 for example, Joseph O'Cain with an American ship, and Russian-supplied native hunters, harvested sea otters from California and the Baja coast from Rosario to Santa Domingo. These southern otter pelts were not as good, but good enough. When he arrived back at Kodiak to meet the Russians he had 11,000 otter pelts his hunters had taken and 700 he had purchased and traded (illegally) from the Spanish. In 1839 otter pelts were still being collected as far south as Cedros Island (300 miles south of San Diego).

American claims to the coast were weak, with only Gray's discovery of the Columbia River, Lewis and Clark, and John Jacob Astor's funding of the construction of Astoria in 1811. Astoria was sold to the British during the War of 1812 but was ultimately reclaimed by the Treaty of Ghent in 1818. Overland fur traders and settlers from America added increasing pressure to the land conflict in the Oregon country and a provisional Oregon government was established by local residents in 1841.

Further north, the American presence faded as the sea otter trade declined and sealing and whaling became more profitable. Interest in the north coast and Alaska was modest even after the purchase of Alaska in 1867. But the discovery of gold in the Yukon (1896) changed everything.

THE SPANISH & MEXICANS

The Treaties of Tordesillas (1494) and Zaragoza (1529) divided the world between Spain and Portugal. This split gave what is now Mexico and the Americas almost entirely to Spain.

Exploration and exploitation were well underway by the time the second treaty was signed. The first explorers of the West Coast were Spanish sailors with a Portuguese captain, Juan Rodríguez Cabrillo in 1542. He coasted California and discovered San Diego harbor. Cabrillo broke his arm while landing on the Channel Islands to aid a shore party that was being attacked. His arm never healed and he eventually died and was buried on San Miguel Island.

Spanish treasure ships also stopped and were shipwrecked in Baja and California during the late 1500s and 1600s. Sebastian Vizcaino sailed the coast in 1602 looking for Monterey Bay and other places where the Philippine treasure ships could find refuge.

Increasing activity by the English and Russian traders and explorers led the Spanish to move north out of the missions in Baja California. The Jesuit priest Miguel Venegas emphasized the Russian risk in a book published in Madrid in 1757. "*...the Russians in future voyages, will come down as low as Cape Blanco: and if California be abandoned by the Spaniards even as far as Cape San Lucas.*" The Baja ports were important stopping points for the treasure ships carrying plunder from the Philippines back to Spain. San Diego was started as a mission and military installation in 1769, with San Francisco following suit in 1776, and Santa Barbara in 1782. The primary goals were colonization; blocking the Russians, Americans and English; income for Spain and the church; and conversion of natives to the Catholic faith. (Not necessarily in that order.)

To further affirm claims, the Spanish naval officer Esteban José Martínez arrived at Nootka Sound in May 1789 and built Fort San Miguel. When the British ship *Argonaut* arrived, a dispute arose between Captain Colnett (who had planned to build a British out-post) and Martínez. This led to the seizure of several British ships. When the news reached Europe, Britain requested compensation but the Spanish government refused. Both sides prepared for war and sought assistance from allies. The crisis was resolved peace-fully but with difficulty through a set of three agreements known

The Spanish made their claim with Fort San Miguel, 1791, but failed to support it.

collectively as the Nootka Conventions (1790–1794). Spain agreed to share some rights to settle along the Pacific Coast but maintained its Pacific claims. This agreement facilitated British expansion as Spain no longer played a role north of California.

In 1784, Vicente Vasadre y Vega proposed a plan to exchange Chinese quicksilver (mercury used for gold refining) for California furs to the Viceroy and King Carlos III. China had a good supply of mercury and a seemingly insatiable demand for sea otter furs, while California and Mexico were short of mercury needed for processing gold ore. Vasadre also highlighted the risk from the growing push to the south by the Russians and English. Instead of returning empty to San Blas from California each year, the ships could bring sea otter pelts to Acapulco for reshipment on the Manila galleons, and from Manila to China for mercury or money. His arguments were well received and on June 2, 1785, King Carlos III ordered that the plan be given careful consideration. Father Lasuén and Governor Fages had high hopes for the project. Vasadre's first collection was encouraging and in just three months of traveling on land and sea he visited nine missions, four presidios, and two pueblos. By the time he left San Diego for San Blas on November 28, he had 1,060 skins.

Sadly, like the British, his effort was derailed by a bureaucracy (in this case the Philippine Company that held trading rights for the Philippines and China.)

In 1785, a royal *cedula* forbade all private trade in furs. American traders (smugglers) were very active and easily found willing customers. They tormented the Spanish administration from 1797–1821, and later the Mexican government. The American ships were well led and armed and felt little fear of the Spanish. In a particularly bold move, the *Lelia Byrd* reached San Diego Bay after buying many furs illegally along the Baja coast in 1803. The *comandante* in San Diego was incensed when the Americans bought still more furs in San Diego. He tried to keep the ship in port but the *Leila Bird* exchanged a few shots with the Spanish Fort Guijarros on

Point Loma and escaped to sea unharmed, having used hostages as protection.

Spain eventually transferred many of its historic territorial claims to the United States in the Adams–Onís Treaty of 1819. Spain continued to control present-day California until 1821, when Mexico proclaimed independence on September 27. Mexican independence changed things yet again. Land grants to officers enabled a lucky few to become ranchers and men of means. The mission system had almost 400,000 cattle, 320,000 sheep, and 60,000 horses by 1830. In 1833 a new governor for California, Jose Figueroa, brought new energy to the area and accelerated the privatization of mission lands. In response, the missions slaughtered more than 100,000 cattle in 1834 to sell the hides and tallow, cashing out before privatization.

American ships transported most of the hides, and along with them, a few furs. Richard Henry Dana was in California in 1835 at the peak of the cow hide trade (see "Two Years Before the Mast"). He employed a mixed group of workers, commenting on the twelve Hawaiians living in a huge Russian bread oven at the beach in San Diego. Point Loma had a large hide preparation area and much firewood was consumed in drying the hides. This is probably when the pine trees were stripped from the point. Hides were the currency of exchange for a time and became known as *California banknotes.*

The maritime trade brought in foreigners and led to settlement pressure as Americans jumped ship, became Catholic, took up Mexican citizenship and married local women.

By the 1830s, a steamship (the *Beaver*) was working the coast out of Astoria, Oregon for the HBC. Accompanied by other sailing ships, it was trading on the Hawaii, northwest coast, and Southern California routes. Much trade was also going from Hawaii to China so diseases from Asia were brought east as well.

THE HAWAIIAN KINGDOMS
Beginning in 1795 King Kamehameha the First consolidated power in a series of wars, and by 1810, he was the undisputed leader of

Hawaii. Fur trade ships from all nations stopped to get water, food, companionship, and supplies, often paying a high price. The fur ships also hired *kanakas* to work on ships and land operations throughout the fur lands.

Women were sometimes romanced, purchased, or abducted for on-ship entertainment. Trading companies established bases in Hawaii, most on the main island at Honolulu and on Oahu, but there were also short-lived Russian outposts on Oahu and Kauai.

The men, ships, and armaments of the fur trade played a critical role in the tribal wars that erupted in Hawaii. Cannons, muskets, and sailing ships changed the balance of power and increased the lethality of war. Venereal diseases, measles, and small pox were brought to Hawaii and communities that had once been the epitome of health and beauty were beset with death and disfiguring diseases. When King Kamehameha the Second traveled to England in 1824 on a whaling ship, one of his goals was to arrange for British protection for his kingdom. While in London both he and his wife succumbed to the measles, limiting the negotiations and further destabilizing the political situation at home when 10-year-old Kamehameha the Third assumed the throne.

CHANGES IN THE LAND AND SEA

The remarkable Steller's sea cow, up to 25 feet long and weighing more than 4 tons, was extinct in 1768, just 27 years after it was first discovered by the Russian explorers in Alaska. The removal of the beaver and otters initiated profound changes in the rivers and coastal waters as ecosystem function and structure were radically changed (see more in Chapter 4). Increasing visits by ships led to tree cutting for masts, spars, ship repair, and fire wood. Cattle and horse drives spread weed seeds across hundreds of new miles of trail. In California, hundreds of thousands of cattle were wild and uncounted. In the drought of 1828–29 an estimated 40,000 mission livestock starved to death. They devastated the rangeland but the carcasses provided food for a much-enlarged grizzly bear population. No market for the beef existed, but the hides (and tallow) were worth exporting and were collected, dried, baled and shipped. More than 1.25 million hides were shipped from California between 1820 and 1845. In Hawaii many of the fur traders switched to carrying sandalwood to China after the sea otter populations were decimated. Traders played off the rivalry among chiefs to get the best prices. Large profits were made, and by 1830, the sandalwood trade had completely collapsed as the best trees were gone.

Summary

The Russians profited early on but the American's economic advantages and unfettered capitalism[16] helped win the struggle for dominance. The British held their own in the interior and everyone else lost. The Spanish (and later Mexicans) were displaced, the Hawaiians were devastated, and the people of the First Nations lost the most. Many critical actions were decided upon by the people who were on the coast, often neglecting laws and morality. As the old Chinese proverb puts it, *"The mountains are high and the emperor is far away."*

The Americans had won the territory with settlement and more efficient enterprises, Oregon City mills 1846.

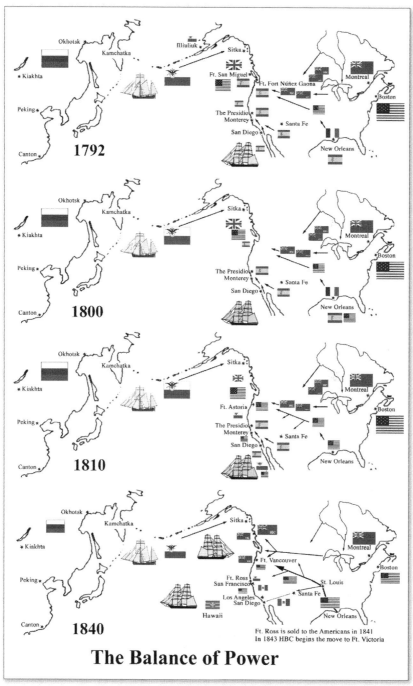

The Balance of Power

These maps reflect the changes in power from 1792–1840.

CHAPTER 2

Fur Trade Economics

*A*lthough the struggle for furs and control of territory was partly political, the action on the front lines was primarily determined by money, profit, and loss.

The economics of the fur trade shifted from year to year and was influenced by political and cultural events from afar. Economic downturns (the Panics of 1792, 1796, 1819, 1825, 1837), many wars, Sweden v/s Russia (1788–1790; 1808–1809), Russia v/s Turkey (1806–1812), France and Spain v/s Portugal (1801), the U.S. v/s

The storm-tossed Fur Coast was dangerous and often deadly.

Britain (1812–1815), and the Napoleonic wars (1800–1815) all affected shipping, financing, tariffs, and market demand. There were also internal conflicts, with fighting from resistance in the Aleutians down to Baja California and the unification wars in Hawaii (1782–1810).

A short overview is followed with more detailed information on the economics of specific furs: sea otter, beaver, and others.

At its peak, the sea otter trade was extremely profitable, risky and often violent. It can be compared to the drug cartels today. The Russians were active first and had the trade to themselves for more than 40 years. After the members of Captain James Cook's expedition discovered the value of sea otter furs in Canton the international race was on. British Captain James Hanna was first on the scene in

1785 out of Macau flying a Portuguese flag.[17] One enthusiastic newspaper reporter in London gushed about his first voyage, *"You will be astonished when I tell you, that the whole out-fit, with the vessel, did not cost them £1,000 and though she was not more than one month on the coast, the furs she collected were sold at Canton for upwards of £30,000."* Not true, but yet it hinted at the opportunity.

Sailing after furs was dangerous. The extended voyages of several years, often around the world or wintering in the North Pacific, were hard on men and ships. Much of the fur trade area was uncharted; the weather could be severe,[18] and some of the ships, captains, and crews were not the best. Ships could also be taken or burned by native people. It was easy to lose money if trading, timing, management and luck were poor. Owners could, and did, lose if the captains cheated (as Captains John Kendrick and Sam Hill apparently did), if fires hit Canton at the wrong time, if ships sank, or if unexpected border closures or import bans hit and stopped trade. The Chinese suspended trade in their fur market ten times between 1744 and 1792. These closures ranged from one day in 1751 to seven years beginning in 1785.

Financial arrangements for fur cruises were highly variable depending on the reputation and skill of the captain and the ownership (captains often owned a share) and the nature of the intended trade. Was it out from Okhotsk to the Pribilof Islands and back? For the early Russian traders, the profits were often 100–200% and sometimes 500–700%.

Later, it could be out and return to Boston on the Golden Round (see map), or back and forth from Canton, Hawaii, to the northwest coast, and back to Canton. The captain, captain/owner, and skilled positions might get six shares or more; each sailor or worker would get just half a share along with typically being overcharged for supplies and food. Natalia Shelikov was an expert at using this to improve company profits. Keep in mind that workers could also reap bigger rewards if not everyone made it back alive.

For British and American ships, the incentives and rewards could be split differently on each leg of the trade. The pay could be straight salary (more common with the British), by a share of the take (as seen with American ships), or some combination thereof. For ships out of Boston the salaries might be only $20–100 per month for the captain (plus a percentage and privilege of space for personal trading), a bit less for the mate and skilled positions, and as low as $5–10 a month for basic seamen. The crew had to purchase supplies from the ship's locker and this often took a good portion of their earnings. The sales to ship crew often yielded a 100% profit for the ship owner.

For a successful cruise the returns could be quite good. In 1799, when the J. & T. Lamb Company paid ordinary seamen $168 to $204 a year, the crew of the Lamb's *Sea Otter* was paid off, each man receiving $500 to $600 each at the end of the two-year cruise. This was after deducting $100–$150 for the supplies most sailors bought from the ship.

Selling a fur in Canton for $20, $50, or $100 could make a big difference to a sailor or captain, and some ship owners allowed them to trade while others fanatically opposed it for cutting into

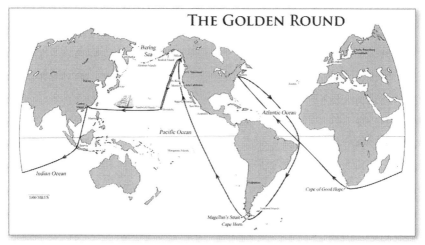

THE GOLDEN ROUND

Some fur traders became very rich. Sailors from Boston became so dominant that all American sailors were called "Boston Men" by some of the First Nations.

their profits. When seaman John Bartlett left the *Massachusetts* in China in 1791, he was paid his $90 salary but had to smuggle his seventeen skins off at night before he could sell them for $600. Captain Metcalfe had been so tight with money that the crew was forced to buy their own fresh water in port and Bartlett was glad to see the last of him.

Losses could be heavy if furs were not well-treated or packed, or if heavy weather soaked the furs. The number of skins wasted is unknown but it would be realistic to believe it to be somewhere between 10–15% at minimum. The Russian ship *Neva* had to toss £40,000 worth of furs overboard on one trip after they rotted, and another vessel lost 100,000 imperfectly cured seal skins that had to be dug out of her hold and sold as manure. The Spanish often had trouble keeping furs in good condition on the voyage to the Philippines or over land to Mexico City.

The Spanish sea otter trade envisioned by Vasadre y Vega in 1786 was stymied by the Philippines Company, a bureaucracy set up by a charter from the Spanish king. In 1799, the formation of the Russian American Company,[19] with a fur monopoly for Alaska, brought new controls and regulations to the fur harvest in the north. It replaced the contentious and ill-mannered private enterprises with more stable but less aggressive management designed to better protect workers and natives. After 1818, it was mandated that the RAC governor had to be an officer in the Russian Navy in another attempt to reduce abuse of natives and *kreols*. This led to better management in many ways, but these officers were not as market-oriented, and profits lagged.

The British fur traders were also up against bureaucracy. The Hudson's Bay Company (founded by a Royal Charter in 1670) was accustomed to government cooperation and intervention and had grown a stable and conservative bureaucracy after more than 100 years. To move furs through to China, the HBC and its rival, the North West Company, had to deal with the East India Company (EIC), which controlled the markets in China, also under a charter from the British Crown. The EIC commonly prohibited fur ships from exporting goods to England from Canton, thus denying them the Golden Round the Americans would enjoy. British ships also had to deal with the South Sea Company (SSC), a weak organization with the charter to manage the Pacific trade. To escape this burden, British fur traders would operate under a foreign flag such as Portugal, Spain, or Austria, trans-ship furs on American vessels, or smuggle furs into China or Macau.

By comparison, the Americans were free to make the best deals possible; they were unhampered by bureaucracy and funded by

Sea otter populations were incredible.

venture capital from small companies and partnerships. A proposal to create a company with a monopoly comparable to the East India Company for fur trades with the Indians, was rejected in 1786 when the Continental Congress expressed the popular opinion that "commercial intercourse between the United States and the Indians would be more prosperous if left unfettered in the hands of private adventurers than if regulated by any system of national complexion."

The Americans became very adept (and at times ruthless) in collecting furs. In 1792 the British sold 77,330 fine furs in Canton and the U.S. sold only 9,579, but by 1801 the Americans landed 444,087 fine fur pieces. These included at least 18,000 sea otter pelts from the Fur Coast. The next year they sold 42,527 sea otter pelts. The Americans ultimately probably took more than 150,000 sea otters to Canton from the western coasts.

Russian ships sailed in very difficult conditions in the North Pacific to get back to Okhotsk. From there the furs had to be trans-shipped at high cost and risk to Kyakhta, Mongolia for sale into China. Spanish ships were often hampered by less able ships, shortages of capable sailors, poor maintenance, and support. They were often ravaged by scurvy. At one point a Spanish ship in Nootka had to take on American and British sailors for the journey home. The surviving Spanish crew certainly appreciated the help, but it landed the captain in deep trouble with his superiors.

British ships tended to be less efficient with more men (including servants), perhaps 25 or more instead of 18 on a comparable American ship. The Americans were typically more highly skilled sailors (few conscripts) and American ships could make three voyages to China for every two with a British ship. By comparison, the American ships also cost less to build, outfit, and insure. This competitive edge took the market away from the British ships.

The cost of goods for trading and operations was also important. Here again, the Americans had an advantage. The cost per ton of getting goods to Sitka was about 585 rubles by land from Petersburg to Okhotsk overland and then by ship to Alaska. It cost just 217 rubles by sea from Kronstadt but it was very slow. The British could bring goods in for about 64 rubles, but the Americans could do it for just 50. This helped give the Americans the edge until they left the northwest coast. The balance of power swung from the Russians to the British to the Americans and then back to the British as the sea furs were depleted.

The beaver was the most important of the many land furs traded. The shift to land furs reduced the profit potential and offered different risks. The demand for beaver skins was primarily driven by the demand for beaver hats and prices were stable for a long time. Beaver were taken or traded in large numbers by the Russians and British but were the mainstay for the American push into the mountain west, southwest and northwest. The shift to silk hats dampened demand for beaver and the price in London tumbled 90% from 27 shillings 6 pence in 1839 to 3s5d in 1846.

THE ECONOMICS OF THE SEA OTTER HARVEST

The sea otter, first known in commerce in 1725, has an exceedingly fine, soft, close fur. A full-grown prime skin pressed before drying can be five to six feet long and twenty-four to thirty inches wide. It is covered with very fine fur, about three-fourths of an inch in length, with a rich jet-black or dark brown glossy surface and a silver color when blown open. The sea otter fur has 850,000–1,000,000 hairs per square inch, the densest fur of any mammal.[20] The fur is not waterproof but the undercoat and longer guard hairs trap a layer of air next to the skin to keep the skin from getting wet.

The Russians discovered the value of the sea otter pelt more than forty years before the Europeans and Americans. Several Russian traders became rich by collecting sea otter pelts from the Aleutian Islands. After the discovery of the value of sea otters with the return of the survivors of the Bering Expedition in 1742, the fur rush was on. From 1743 to 1800, more than 150 Russian ventures were outfitted to the Commander and Aleutian Islands and the Alaskan coast. In 1787 alone, 25 Russian vessels manned by 1,000 men were active. These small private enterprise companies were supposed to purchase permits from the Russian government to acquire furs (and at times had to take along an official government agent). The Russian Empire benefitted from taxes (10%) and duties, fur tribute from the islanders, and a 20–25% fee when the skins were traded into China at the Kyakhta crossing. At times during the latter 1700s, the China trade represented about one-half (by value) of Russia's foreign trade and furs were an important part of that trade.

The early Russian ventures often worked for shares of the often-substantial profits. The captain or captain/owner and skilled positions might get six shares or more while each sailor or worker would get just half a share or less, and natives from Kamchatka or Siberia even less. The sailors would usually be charged for all supplies and food used. Natalia Shelikov was an expert at employing this system to improve company profits. Some men returned year after year and reaped a very rich harvest. Nikifor Trapeznikov made or sponsored 23 voyages (1774–1786) and made 1.5 million rubles, about $289 million in today's dollars. Four other traders made more than a million rubles.

The take of sea otters from 1743 through 1798 was on the order of 250,000 skins worth ten million rubles. After the formation of the Russian American Company (RAC) the slaughter continued, with 72,894 sea otters taken from 1797 to 1821; 25,416 from 1822 to 1841; and 25,899 from 1842 to 1862. Much of the hunt was done from *baidarkas* working in teams with a Russian or *kreol* supervisor. In the early days of the RAC a male native working in Sitka received only clothing and upkeep for his services. In 1804, the RAC specified that the hunter should get 10 rubles[21] for a sea otter pelt that the company might sell for 250 rubles in China. In 1810, natives were paid 60–150 rubles a year, *kreol*[22] apprentices 180–450, and navigators as much as 2,000–2,450 rubles. In 1817, Baranov was still able to hire a number of Aleut men for just 60 rubles a year. If a man died while working as a hunter on an American or British ship, the ship owner was required to pay the family 1,250 rubles, but they didn't always comply. The small investors, *promyshlenniki*, and sailors from Russian ships had to sell their furs at a discount in Kamchatka. Enterprises with greater resources would sell them in Okhotsk, or if they could manage it and the border was open, in Kyakhta. In 1760 a sea otter skin was worth 20 rubles in Okhotsk and 40 in Kyakhta. In 1772 a prime fur would have brought $40 in Kamchatka and $140 in Kyakhta.

After Cook's expedition revealed the opportunity of profit to the rest of the world from sea otter skins, ships started to arrive from all over. The first was the British *Sea Otter* out of Macau under James Hanna in 1785 flying a Portuguese flag to avoid taxes and regulations and ease entry into the Chinese market. He obtained 560 pelts during a short visit and for a reported investment of around $17,000 and a month on the coast, he made more than $24,000 (about $700,000 today). This was enough to attract new investors and venture capital.

Ships on the NW Coast

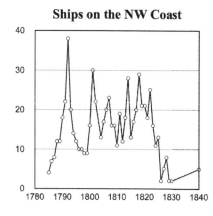

As many as 500 ships visited the North Pacific and California coasts between 1774 and 1820, not all after furs. Most flew the Stars and Stripes, followed by the Union Jack, RAC and Russian flags, and the red-and yellow-striped flag of Spain. In 1786, the French commander, the Compte de La Perouse, gave the money (perhaps $10,000), he made from the sale of the thousand sea otter skins his expedition collected to his 100 sailors. Between 1790 and 1818 traders carried an estimated 300,000 sea otter pelts to China from the northwest coast.

By 1800, the Americans were on the rise in the fur trade. From June 11, 1800 to January 9, 1803 reports put the number of sea otters delivered to Canton by Americans at 34,357 worth $695,000 dollars at the time or about $18 million in today's dollars.[23] In 1802 the Russians took only about 10,000 otters. From 1804 to 1837 American vessels exported more than 150,000 sea otter pelts to market at Canton. With the price of a pelt over the same period averaging between $20–100, the trade netted millions of dollars and made some people very rich.

For example, the 1794–96 cruise of the *Despatch* reported $25,563 for expenses and duties and grossed $51,541, netting $25,978—a 100% profit. In 1796, the *Ruby* under Captain Charles Bishop, bought furs for fifty cents worth of goods on the coast that brought twelve dollars on the Chinese market for a 2400% markup. The *Ruby* collected 864 otter skins, 47 large sea otter cloaks (cutsarks) of three skins each, 483 sea otter tails, and 169 other pieces of sea otter skin.

The market peaked quickly and prices declined as competition increased. By 1800, American ship captains told Baranov that they had to get at least 1500 skins to make a profitable voyage. It was said that only two of the six ships that took skins to Canton in 1800 did so.

The voyages of the *Atahualpa* (1801–03), *Guatimozin* (1801–02), and *Vancouver* (1802–04), owned by Theodore Lyman and Associates, may have returned only half of their total cost (nearly $90,000) as a result of mistakes in merchandising and management.

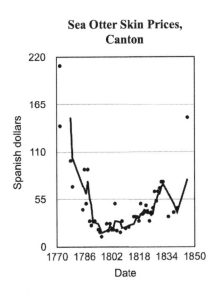

Sea Otter Skin Prices, Canton

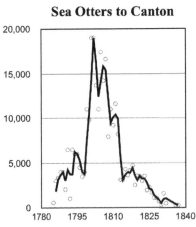

Sea Otters to Canton

In contrast, Captain William Sturgis from Boston reported in 1800 that it was still possible to make $150,000 on an investment of $40,000 on the Golden Round (Boston, NW Coast, Canton, Boston). On one trip he managed to collect 6,000 sea otters valued at about $120,000. This was quite good, but another firm's investment of $50,000 gave a gross return of $284,000. From 1808–09 John Suter and the *Pearl* collected 6,000 otter skins worth about $180,000. His net worth would have been about $32 million in today's dollars. Strong incentive, indeed.

One of the keys to making a profit was having what the native people wanted. This shifted over time from copper to iron to guns and powder. William Sturgis was one of the best merchandisers and listened carefully to learn what his customers wanted. In 1804 he brought 5,000 ermine skins bought for 30¢ each to the NW coast. Paying just 5 ermines per sea otter pelt he obtained 560 prime sea otter in a single forenoon. Skins worth more than $50 each in Canton cost him just $1.50. He traded all of his ermines at the same rate for a gross profit of $80,000. A capable captain and skillful trader, he quickly became rich enough to hire others to do the cruising. Later ships tried to match his success with ermines but in less than two years the market had changed so drastically that a hundred ermines wouldn't buy a single otter skin.

In some cases, the items traded for sea otters were of native manufacture. One trader estimated that the 192 half-inch thick elk hide armor *clamons* he had acquired from the Chinooks would fetch him 677 prime sea otter pelts from the natives of the Queen Charlotte Islands. In return for the *clamons*, the Chinook received just ten pounds of powder, four muskets, 304 copper rods, 73 tea kettles, and 16 pounds of sheet copper.[24]

By 1810, it was even more difficult (but still not impossible) to make a profit on sea otter. The cost of acquiring furs rose as otters became scarcer. Sea otter pelts that may once have traded for some beads, a pot, or an iron dagger, might now cost a blanket, musket, or lead and powder. As tribes armed themselves, the demand for muskets, lead and powder increased and the suppliers responded to market demand. With rising competition for fewer available pelts, the price of sea otter furs rose even higher, from a low of five pelts for a musket, to one pelt per musket and then to 3–6 muskets per pelt. At a cost of a few dollars each, the musket value might approximate the value of the pelt in Canton. Captain William Sturgis reported seeing prices paid on the coast for furs exceeding the value of the pelts. On the NW coast in 1827, each ship returned with no more than 150 sea otters costing them $30 each—about what they would sell for in Canton. This led to more harvesting of land furs, especially beaver, and a switch to other marine mammals including fur seals, sea lions, and whales.

The last gasp of the sea otter trade was in California, although it was a relatively small portion of the overall sea otter industry. The California sea otter trade began in 1784[25] when a Spanish expedition headed by Vicente Vasadre y Vega traded abalone shells, beads, and metal articles to the natives for sea otter pelts. Vega organized and expanded the sea otter trade with furs sent to Mexico for tanning and then on to China in exchange for quicksilver needed in

the Mexican gold mines. An annual galleon that sailed from Acapulco to Manila in 1783 carried over 700 sea otter skins.

By 1785 otter skins had become important enough for Governor Pedro Fages to issue a regulation punishing anyone except missionaries who traded in furs. Military and

Pressure to meet hunt goals led to many hunters lost at sea.

civilians didn't heed the new law and were often guilty of cheating the natives or simply seizing the furs and then demanding payment from the missions. In January 1786, a formal plan for this trade was approved by Viceroy Bernardo de Galvez and Governor Fages. In August 1786, Vega arrived in California with a monopoly for the entire business and substantial financial backing. Governor Fages made the scheme public on August 29th, making the missionaries Vega's agents to help him get all the pelts. Skins collected by the missions were to be handed over to the presidio commanders and then channeled to Vega. The set prices ranged from ten pesos for first-class skins, which had to be of at least 42 inches long, black in color, and cured. During his three-month stay, Vega collected 1,060 pelts, including some from Baja California.

The missions were obliged to pay seven silver pesos for pelts that already belonged to them by law. Even when pelts were legally hunted the missions lacked the cash reserves to pay for them. In 1789, Purisma, Santa Barbara, and San Buenaventura all sent more than 70 skins but Don Francisco de Paula Tamariz estimated that about 2,500–3,000 furs were taken in California each year. Most went out on Boston ships that could pay a much higher price, even if it was illegal.

In 1790, Vega's project was dropped by royal decree when he was blocked by the Philippine Company which had a royal monopoly on trade with China. The California sea otter fur trade was never fully realized because the Spanish and later Mexican governments and bureaucrats never really understood the opportunity. They restricted the harvest, drove missions and soldiers to trade illegally, and paid such low prices (if they paid anything) that natives and settlers were unwilling to hunt otters.

The turning point in the California sea otter trade came in 1803 when Joseph O'Cain negotiated an innovative hunting strategy with Baranov and the RAC. Russia would supply hunters and *baidarkas*, and O'Cain would provide transport on his ship, the *O'Cain*. Fur profits would be shared 50:50. O'Cain returned to Kodiak with 1,800 sea otter pelts: 1,100 caught and 700 bartered with the Spanish.

In 1806 the deals were repeated with even more ships, *baidarkas*, and hunters. This time O'Cain was captain of the *Eclipse*. The *O'Cain,* now under Captain Jonathan Winship, continued far down the coast past San Quintin to Cedros Island off Baja California. These ships deposited hunters on islands and coastal inlets, blanketing the Baja coast with hunters, *baidarkas*, and female skinners. The *Peacock* with Captain Kimball established a base at Bodega Bay and sent dozens of hunters in *baidarkas* into San Francisco Bay where Georg Heinrich von Langsdorff noted, "*the valuable sea-otter was swimming in numbers about the bay.*" The *Peacock* returned to Sitka after six months with over 1,200 otter pelts. In 1806/07 the *Mercury* was trading on the California coast and obtained 107 skins from the Mission in Santa Barbara worth $692; 300 skins worth $2,500 from San Luis Obispo; and six worth $58 from San Gabriel Mission. The missions accepted about half the price in goods, reducing the cost to the traders. In return, the *contrabandistas* provided much-needed supplies and cash for the missions.

Captain William Heath Davis of the *Mercury* preferred to buy furs from the missions while dispatching small groups of Aleut hunters in the vicinity of the more remote missions. The *Mercury* left California in August 1806, with a cargo of almost 3,000 sea otter pelts. The *O'Cain* departed for Russian Alaska with over 200 souls on board, pelts valued at $136,310 in Canton, and two pregnant Aleut women who gave birth during the voyage north.

Captain John Ebbets reported to John Jacob Astor at the end of 1810, *"The killing (of) Sea Otter in California has been attended with little danger and much profit."* The California sea otter fur trade was most profitable and productive between 1803 and 1816. The profits derived in Canton from these American-Russian ventures remained high with prices averaging over $25 per sea otter pelt in Canton. A big catch could provide a veritable fortune for the traders able to cash in.

But it would prove to be too little too late; after the Mexican Revolution in 1821, the government opened its arms to trade but there were few sea otters left. In 1821 the RAC began to hunt on halves with the Mexican authorities with little profit. In June 1822, the English brig *John Begg* arrived at Monterey from Lima with a small cargo of trade goods. Hugh McCulloch and William Edward Petty Hartnell wanted to establish a branch of the firm of John Begg & Company of Lima, Peru, under the name of McCulloch & Hartnell, in Monterey. The plan they submitted to Governor Sola was approved and on June 11, Sola wrote to Father Payeras, the Prefect of the Missions, outlining the plan. On June 12, Father Payeras addressed his colleagues, the mission padres, on the advantages of free trading. On June 20, notice was sent to all missions, notifying

Rafts of sea otters in the hundreds, became rafts of tens and then they were gone.

them of the official prices arranged. Similar notices were sent to the military *comandantes*, announcing that the pueblos and ranchos could sell all the fur, hides, tallow, and other produce they pleased at the same prices. The agreement went into effect in January 1823 and Hartnell and McCulloch conducted an extensive trade with the California missions, exchanging sea otter, beaver and other furs, cow hides and tallow, foodstuffs, and other goods. Hartnell converted to Catholicism in 1824, married María Teresa de la Guerra in 1825, and became a Mexican citizen in 1830. It was too late for the Mexicans to profit much from sea otter skins. The otters were gone.

By the late 1820s the California sea otter hunt resembled a contest to find and kill the last otter. George Nidever teamed up with Allen Light (an African-American hunter nicknamed the "Black Steward") and a Hawaiian to scour the once-plentiful otter grounds of the Santa Barbara Channel. They used long rifles and bagged a couple dozen sea otters. Nidever remembered with incredulity the early times when sea otters were so plentiful they could be killed with spears. However, there were still furs to be found in more remote areas. The *Bolivar Liberator* managed to bring in 400 sea otter skins in 1836 with twenty Tongass Haida hunters and *baidarkas*.

More than 45,000 sea otter pelts can be counted in records of the ships on the California coast. Many ships did not list numbers and other ships were never even noted as they avoided Spanish officials. The total take was probably closer to 60,000 to 80,000 including Spanish efforts. Many otters were also killed by hunters but not recovered. The California sea otter populations were almost completely destroyed, with the once-extensive populations of Baja, and Alta, California reduced to mere remnants struggling for survival.

Over the full period of the sea otter hunts more than 700,000, and perhaps a million, sea otters were killed in the rush for riches. Even after the populations were severely depleted, the hunts continued. From 1868 to 1905 another 100,000 skins were taken. Year after year the populations sank, but London's yearly sea otter sale in 1891 was still estimated to be worth $450,000 with an average price of about $250 per skin and a high of $1,300. Sea otter furs were sold on to Russia for noblemen's coat collars and some skins were also used for clothing in England, France, the United States and Canada.

At the end, only about a thousand sea otters survived along the thousands of miles of coastline. A small group of about fifty otters tucked away in the rugged Big Sur coastline near Bixby Creek in California were the sole survivors of the southern populations. As the Sea Otter Range Map in Chapter 4 shows, sea otters have returned to many islands and areas where they were once driven to extinction. On the western coast of the U.S., the sea otter populations have grown but are still but a shadow of their former selves and still missing in Oregon and Baja California (for more detail, see Ecological Impacts of the Fur Trade, Chapter 4).

In modern times the poaching of sea otters on the Bering Islands is still a problem. The Commander Islands' Nature Preserve doesn't have adequate resources to provide protection for the sea otters. In recent years an estimated 200–300 animals (perhaps more) have been taken illegally. The price of a sea otter skin on the black market in Petropavlovsk ranges from $500–1,200. Most of the skins go to China and South Korea.

THE ECONOMICS OF BEAVER

Beaver are large rodents that can reach 4–6 feet in length and weigh 90 pounds or more. The beautiful and tragic flaw of the beaver lies in its magnificent fur ranging in color from yellow, brown, to almost black. The fur is very dense with guard hairs over soft underfur. The hairs interlock to help protect the beaver from cold water by retaining air. The interlocking hairs made the beaver an ideal source of fiber for felting and particularly for felt hats. The beaver also produces a yellowish secretion, castoreum, in two sacks between the pelvis and the tail bone. This was used as a lure by trappers. It was also commercially collected and used as a scent enhancer in perfumes and as a food additive. It was considered an almost magical remedy in traditional medicine.

Beaver pelts came either as dry raw pelts (parchment, *sec*) or coat (fat, *gras*) furs that had been used in native garments. The guard hairs were worn off on coat furs used in clothing; this made them more flexible and easier to process for felt. A "made beaver" was one "coat" beaver. In the early years, coat beaver were more valuable than parchment. Parchment furs became more valuable

once the technique of carotting[26] was developed to remove the guard hairs. Beaver fur quality was generally lower for furs from the south and toward the coast with better quality in the north and mountains.

The demand for beaver felt for hats created the market.

The fur was best in late fall to early spring, but trappers in the field often kept taking furs even when the quality was lower. Many grades of beaver were noted and the quality and size determined the price they would bring. Beaver pelts were generally shipped in 90-pound packs, typically of 45–60 skins. The prices in London for beaver were relatively stable for decades until a precipitous drop of 90% around 1840 when silk hats became the rage.

The reduction in European beaver populations from over-hunting to support a fashion trend favoring felt hats around 1800 drove a new rush for beaver skins. Beaver gained new attention in the west as the more valuable sea otters became scarce. The North American beaver (*Castor canadensis*) was once common and widely distributed with populations estimated as high as 400 million before European settlement, trapping, hunting, and habitat loss. They were successful in habitats as hot as the Colorado and Gila Rivers in the deserts of Arizona and California, down to the Gulf of California and to the far north of Alaska and Canada. Beaver could be found in most rivers, wetlands, and estuaries from what is now the Mexican border to the Yukon. Beaver are easy to find, stationary, and thus easy to trap. They reproduce slowly and are very vulnerable to heavy hunting pressure.

The Russian private venture companies, and after 1799, the Russian American Company, relied on native trappers and hunters to bring beaver furs to their outposts. The beaver skins collected by the Russians might go out on a Boston ship, or they might go west to Okhotsk and from there to St. Petersburg or Kyakhta and on to China. The Russian's beaver trade faced considerable disadvantages just as they had with sea otter furs. It cost more to get goods to the outposts, the quality of goods for trade was lower, and the travel needed to get furs to market was more challenging and costlier. Even so, the Russian American Company collected more than 200,000 beaver pelts from Alaska and the Northwest Coast from 1798–1842.

When the American captain Robert Gray first interacted with the Chinooks on the Columbia River in 1792 he noted, "*Shifted the Ship's birth to her Old Station abrest the Village Chinoak, command'd by a cheif name Polack. This River in my opinion, wou'd be a fine place for to sett up a Factory.*[27] *The Indians are very numerous, and appear'd very civill (not even offering to steal). during our short stay we collected 150 Otter, 300 Beaver, and twice the Number of other land furs.*"

The native people readily adapted to thinking of the value of trade goods in Made Beaver equivalents. Many already had extensive trading networks and their bargaining skills often frustrated traders. The trading companies were concerned with the bottom line, operating costs, profit margins, and return on investments. However they operated, the companies' success depended on how much they needed to pay out in trade goods to obtain furs or to pay trappers, how much it cost to transport furs to market, and how much they would bring.

The Hudson's Bay Company and its rival the North West Company were soon established on the coast and west of the mountains after beaver. However, as Duncan McGillivray of the NWC wrote in 1808, "*The trade as it is carried on at present beyond the mountains, instead of getting any profit, is a very considerable loss to the Company, as the furs did not pay the transport to Montreal where they were shipped.*" The 3000-mile overland carry and paddle from the Columbia River to Eastern Canada was costly and slow.

Much of the HBC beaver hunting in the West was done by imported company trappers rather than indigenous hunters. Trappers included French voyageurs, Cree, Iroquois, Ojibway, Mohawk, Mohicans, and others from the East. These men were already skilled in the use of steel traps for catching beaver. The resourceful *kanakas* from Hawaii also adapted quickly.

All of the companies, ships, trading posts and gatherings offered opportunities for free trappers. These men worked as private con-tractors and were paid only if they brought in furs. The companies would often advance them traps and supplies on loans or for a share of their catch. The HBC fur brigades often included both *engages* (salaried men) and free trappers. They traveled in large groups for security and typically the wives and children went along for the 6-month winter trapping parties. In 1830, John Work's brigade included 37 men, 4 hired servants, a slave, 2 youths, 29 women and 45 children (22 boys, 23 girls) for a total of 114 souls. The women were essential to treat the beaver skins because it took at least thirty minutes for a skilled worker to process a skin, and they were some-times trapping 70–80 a day.

John Jacob Astor's effort to create an American fur company in Oregon in 1810 failed despite good planning and a two-pronged approach. The sea-going party under the martinet Captain Thorn cost the company a ship, trade goods, and the lives of many men. The overland party was not well led and suffered greatly, leaving a trail of starving wanderers. They did well simply to survive until they were rescued. Astor's trading post on the Columbia was sold to the British during the War of 1812, but his efforts helped stimulate investment and activity by the HBC and NWC.

Prospects for the region had seemed limited to the HBC until the North West Company's final shipment of Columbia furs to Canton made almost £12,000. This profit benefited the newly merged HBC-NWC company of 1821. In September 1822, a proposal for the extension of trade, economic diversification, and the opening of a direct trade to the west coast was made to the HBC management, and accepted. The economics were good once shipping could go west to the coast and to London or China by ship instead of east over the Rockies and then by a long canoe and boat trip to Montreal. Profits were good. The HBC operations on the Snake River in 1826 collected 2,188 beaver pelts worth more than £4,000 at a cost of just £1,500. A beaver skin costing the company just a few shillings in trade goods could be worth 30–40 shillings in London and about as much in China.

Foreign ships on the NW coast, primarily American, were also getting up to 10,000 beaver pelts a year. This is as many as the HBC was getting from the New Caledonia District and half as many as it was getting from the entire Columbia Department. In 1831 the *Owhyhee,* under Captain John Dominis, returned to Boston with 8,000–9,000 beaver skins, and many lesser furs. The American vessels were siphoning off furs that should, in the HBC's view, have been going to their inland posts but there was not much they could do about it. The Yankee competitors were also raising native expectations for the trade value for their furs. The higher prices the Boston ships could pay for skins forced the HBC to follow suit. One veteran complained that the price of beaver had risen fivefold on the coast during the 1820s because of increased competition.

Each HBC fur post was charged for trade goods and supplies, set at the London invoice price plus expenses. The costs were set by the governor and committee. Given these costs, each fur trade outpost developed its own standard of trade to relate all types of furs and trade goods to the "made-beaver" currency. The goods exchanged to obtain the fur were typically calculated at cost (including transit) plus 50%, so profits were made in several ways. Standards of Trade in effect for the HBC's far-flung trading region were often restrictive, slowed trade, and reduced competitiveness with the Americans.

For a 3-point blanket costing 10 shillings, a trapper might bring in a prime beaver pelt worth 10 shillings at the post. It looked like an even trade, but the trader paid less than 6 shillings for the blanket, including transit costs, and would then sell the pelt in London, New Orleans, or Boston to fur brokers for 30–40 shillings. The fur then went onward to hat makers or tailors in London, Russia or France.

How much was a Made Beaver worth to the natives and trappers? Prices varied with location as a result of the distances and difficulty of supplying remote outposts. They also varied by the competitive situation of each outpost, with an allowance to give higher prices to take furs from competitors. The HBC 1830 Standard of Trade in New Caledonia[28] illustrates the impact of distance. In this remote department, the HBC paid only a few shillings for a beaver skin worth 33 shillings in London. It was profitable even after the higher transport costs from these remote outposts were subtracted.

LIST 1
Trade value in New Caledonia

Item	Made Beaver
trade gun	20
coat	6
a foot of tobacco	1
a gallon kettle	1
small axe	1
two gills of powder	1
one pound of shot	1

When free trappers were able to trade to ships and other companies they were paid much more. In 1836, a made beaver skin was worth 10 shillings in the Columbia Department. A free trapper might receive a credit of 40 shillings for four beaver pelts, buy a gun for 20 shillings, and still have credit left on the books. HBC made even more money on "essential items" like gun flints. A trapper might end up paying one made beaver for two dozen flints that cost the company just 24 pence.

Beaver were over-harvested in the West by the British in a successful attempt to create a fur desert to slow American expansion and minimize land claims.

Beaver hunts in California were initially very effective, but American, Russian and British ships had largely cleared beaver from the northern California coast before any records were kept. The Hudson Bay Company kept good records of their trading activities and most have survived. We know that Thomas McKay trapped 735 beaver and otter on just two small tributaries of the Klamath River. The HBC sent large fur brigades south to California during most years from 1826–1843. In 1829, Alexander R. McLeod reported, *"Beaver is become an article of traffic on the Coast as at the Mission of St. Joseph* (now near Fremont) *alone upwards of Fifteen hundred Beaver Skins were collected from the natives at a trifling value and sold to Ships at 3 Dollars."* Most of the tributaries to San Francisco Bay were good beaver habitat, with trapping on Alameda Creek, the Napa and Sonoma Rivers, Coyote Creek, and many others. In 1829, Thomas McKay and the Hudson's Bay Company men took 4,000 beaver skins on the shores of San Francisco Bay. Ten years later the southern party from the HBC under Michel Laframboise trapped 2,700 beaver in the Sacramento-San Joaquin Delta.

The beaver take of the Columbia Department of the Hudson's Bay Company, with territory throughout Oregon, Washington, northern California, and British Columbia, peaked in 1833 at 21,290 pelts. More than 400,000 were taken from 1820–1840. The American trappers also made great inroads on the California beaver, working over the Sierras and the Sacramento and San Joaquin drainages. Beaver were found as far south as San Diego, where the newspaper as late as 1889 reported, *"A beaver weighing forty pounds was on exhibition on Fifth Street yesterday, having been trapped by Joe McCord, who lives north of the city. It was the largest specimen ever taken in this section."*

The operations of the North West Company, British ship traders, and American trading are less well understood. Many of these

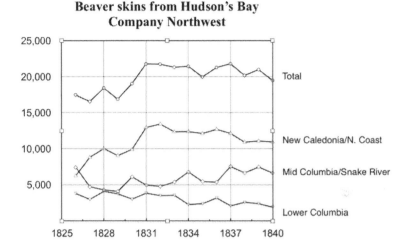

Beaver skins from Hudson's Bay Company Northwest

beaver furs went to China. Much of the American trapping and trading was illegal and so was unreported and the Americans were also good at smuggling furs into China. American trappers usually operated in smaller parties of all men and would sell furs to a ship at the coast, a trading post, at the rendezvous, in Santa Fe, or back in St. Louis.

American traders often offered much more for furs than the HBC and many skins were diverted to the mountain fur rendezvous and other trading outlets for these higher prices. In 1825 American traders from the Missouri, a smaller party from Santa Fe, and a large party under Peter Skene Ogden of the HBC in Oregon collided near Salt Lake. Ogden's men had collected many beaver skins. American Johnston Gardiner (see profile in Tenacity, Volume 2 of this series) offered three times as much in trade as the HBC company policy would let Ogden pay. Many deserted but it was remarkable that any stayed with Ogden. The Americans managed to pick up 700 pelts worth more than $5,000 in St. Louis.

American fur companies were rapidly working their way west from the Missouri River. The Spanish, and later Mexican, fur trappers were working north from Santa Fe. As early as 1810 the Missouri Fur Company reached far to the west and built an outpost at the

The American push for beaver pelts came from the East.

Three Forks of the Missouri. This was good beaver country but the men were harassed by hostile natives and the post was abandoned. The mountain fur trade really took off after the Ashley-Henry Company increased efforts to reach further west in 1822. In 1824 his men brought in 1,000 beaver skins. He realized that taking the goods to the trappers in the mountains would be more economical than maintaining posts where the trappers had to come and the storied beaver rendezvous was born.

Although the iconic fur trade rendezvous started by Ashley lasted just 15 years, from 1825 to 1840, they provided the drive to clear the mountains of beaver. These wild events were accompanied by steady westward movement of trading posts. More than 150 would be scattered throughout the west. They would continue to trade for beaver and other fur-bearing mammals even after the collapse in beaver prices.

In 1826 a made beaver was worth between $4–7 at the rendezvous and Ashley was selling goods as follows:

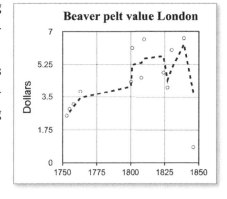

LIST 2
Rendezvous prices 1826

Item	Price
Gunpowder, pound	$ 1.50
Shot, pound	$ 1.25
Flints, dozen	$ 0.50
Knife	$ 0.75
Gun	$ 24
Blanket, 3 pt.	$ 9
Scarlet Cloth, yard	$ 6
Beaver Traps	$ 9
Tobacco, pound	$ 3
Coffee, pound	$ 1.25
Beads, pound	$ 3
The big moneymaker was rum at $13.50 a gallon!	

Trapper Daniel Potts noted that the actual costs paid by trappers were often higher, with gun powder going for up to $2.50 a pound, coffee at $2 a pound, 3-point blankets at $15 each, scarlet cloth at $10 per yard, and horses from $150 to even $500. A good quality rifle might be $30 and a good pistol the same or a bit more. Printed fabric was about 30¢ per yard, but a pierced broach could cost $3 and a silk handkerchief $3.50. With yearly salaries for the contracted trappers ranging from $200–$400, it is apparent that even a successful trapper was not necessarily making much money. If you lost a horse, drank too much, bought too many gewgaws for your country wife, or lost traps or guns to the natives, you could work hard and not break even. A free trapper could make a good profit if he could stay alive, trap effectively, avoid thefts, and get his skins to market.

The records of the American, Spanish, and Mexican fur trappers and traders are limited. They were all eagerly seeking beaver pelts and determined to use them to help define their territorial claims. The American beaver fur businesses peaked in the 1830s with tens of thousands of beaver taken from the western rivers and shipped down to the coast, or more commonly to St. Louis or New Orleans. Indian Agent Thomas J. Dougherty estimated the beaver take on the Missouri River drainages at 375,000 from 1815–1830.

The California beaver were rapidly reduced by the HBC hunting parties from Oregon and American trappers from the east. The total take by all parties in California appears likely to have been about 40,000 beaver.

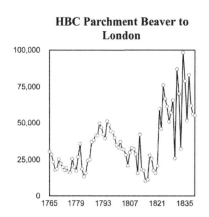

HBC FUR TRAPPERS ROUTES TO CALIFORNIA

By the 1840s beaver populations were considerably reduced throughout the west. From the Colorado River to Alaska, beaver had been over-harvested and wiped out in many areas. The shift to silk hats reduced demand and market prices. The value of a prime skin dropped from 27 shillings 6 pence in 1839 to just 3 shillings 5 pence in the 1840s. The HBC Columbia Department took 20,970 beaver in 1839 and only 12,958 in 1846 as prices dropped.

The total number of beaver taken across the west will never be known because there are too many missing pieces. British trapper Peter Skene Ogden once bragged to the American Jedidiah Smith that he had taken 85,000 beaver worth $600,000 from just the Snake River drainages. In 18 years, the Russians took in more than 40,000 beaver from just one fort in northern Alaska.

The Americans were in the game as well with John Dominis and the *Owyhee* returning to London with 9,000 beaver in 1831. If we consider the HBC,

HBC Parchment Beaver to London

NWC, RAC and other efforts, it seems likely that well more than a million beaver (and perhaps 2+ million) were killed. The catastrophic effects this would have on the landscape are described in Chapter 4.

When sea otters became scarce more attention was focused on beaver. The Russians, British, Spanish and Americans all participated in the beaver trade. Once again the Americans had cost and management advantages and made good use of them. Prices in London and China were relatively stable for many decades and well-managed operations could make money. Trappers and traders were less likely to get rich but the high-level managers like George Simpson and John Jacob Astor did. The price collapse in 1839 gave the beaver a reprieve. Hunting continued but beaver populations gradually recovered in much of British Columbia and Alaska. In the western U.S. and Rocky Mountains, the many areas that need beaver are still missing them (see chapter 4).

THE ECONOMICS OF OTHER FURS

Sea otters and beaver were by far the most important drivers of the fur trade, but traders and trappers would take virtually anything with fur that could be caught and sold, from moles and skunks to polar bears. In 1770, for example, Aphanassei Otcheredin's share from an Alaska hunt included 656 black foxes and 1,250 red fox skins.

Gregorii Shelikov was the first trader to deal extensively in fur seals and took 70,000 in four years from the Commander Islands. More than 100,000 a year may have been taken on the Pribilof Islands in the late 1700s. In 1817 alone, an estimated 60,000 fur seals worth about a dollar each were killed on the Pribilof Islands.

The RAC listed 1.7 million fur seals shipped from 1797–1842. When the American ship *Albatross* sailed from the coast for the Hawaiian Islands in October 1811, she had to break up some of her water casks and shift her spare hemp cables to the deck to make room for 73,000 fur seal skins from the Farallon Islands, as well as

**Northern Fur Seal
Harvest Pribilofs**

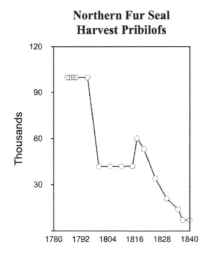

639 sea otter skins, 248 beaver, and a variety of other skins valued at more than $157,000 ($4 million today) in Canton. Two other ships were also working the Farallon Islands that year and an estimated 150,000 seals were killed in just three years. After 1812 the RAC from Fort Ross maintained a hunting outpost on the Farallons.[29]

The 18th and 19th centuries saw a massive slaughter of fur seals wherever they were found from the Antarctic to the Arctic. More than 6 million seals were killed. Populations declined rapidly as this chart of the Pribilofs shows. The majority of the sealers were from Britain and New England. They took fur seals first (for the fur) and later elephant seals (for the oil).

The most important markets were in England, the U.S., and Canton where the furs were valued for hats and other clothing. Prices varied considerably but in Canton a seal skin might bring a dollar. In New York the value ranged from 25¢ to $10. The markets for elephant seal oil were mainly in New York and London, with a value of about 40¢ a gallon in New York.

Furs from seals soon outnumbered the otter and beaver skin imports that had previously been favored by U.S. traders. By the turn of the eighteenth century the market was saturated with fur seals, and prices and imports gradually declined. By the early 1830s the trade to Canton ceased.

The North Pacific Seal Convention of 1911 cowritten by artist and early environmentalist Henry Wood Elliott provided some protection for the Northern Fur Seals and sea otters. Sea lions, other seals, and marine mammals didn't gain much more protection until the Marine Mammal Protection Act of 1972 was passed.

The Guadalupe Fur Seal, *Arcto-cephalus townsendi,* was hunted almost to extinction before scientists even knew they existed. They were found on the islands off the Baja coast, the Channel Islands, and the Farallons, and were not identified as a distinct species until 1897. The original population has been estimated as high as 200,000. At least 16,913 were taken from Guadalupe Island and its vicinity by American companies from 1806–1894; in 1892 only seven were seen on Guadalupe Island. The virtual extermination of this species was the work first of the Russians and then Yankee sailors and their native hunters. The ruins of sealing posts can still be seen on the island.

Sea lions were heavily hunted at times for their meat, fur, skins, oil, and various other products. Sea lions became so scarce in the north that sea lion skins for *baidarkas* had to be imported from California. Extensive commercial killing of California sea lions for their blubber (for oil), hides and penises[30] was carried out in the 19th and early 20th centuries. In the 19th century sea lion whiskers sold for a penny apiece for use as tobacco-pipe cleaners. In the early 1900s sea lions were killed and bountied because fishermen blamed them for stealing fish.

Sea lion hunts decimated herds.

Elephant seals were slaughtered wholesale from about 1818–1869 for the oil that could be rendered from their blubber. This oil was used for lamps and lubrication even though it was not as good as whale oil. The meat and skins also had some value. The hunt was so intense that elephant seals were thought to be extinct by the end of the 1800s.

The RAC aggregated total of shipments over 45 years suggest the surprising toll the fur trade took on other fur-bearing creatures.

LIST 3
Fur-Harvests
Harvests Russian American Company from 1797–1842

Foxes	192,456
Polar foxes	109,948
Sables	32,964
River otters	29,442
Minks	20,283
Bears	6,957
Lynx	5,642
Wolverines	2,715
Wolves	322
Walrus tusks[31]	146 tons
Baleen	83.4 tons

The HBC was also taking other furs. Between 1769 and 1868 the HBC exports for sale in London from North America [32] included the skins of 1,507,240 mink at 5–20 shillings;[33] 1,240,571 marten at 10–20 shillings; 1,052,051 lynx worth 10–40 shillings; 891,091 fox at 10–20 shillings; 467,549 wolf at 5–120 shillings; 288,016 bear at 100–200 shillings; 275,032 badger worth 6–20 shillings; and 68,694 wolverines 10–30 shillings. There were also more than a million deer skins worth about 25¢ each and 1.6 million seal skins worth $1 each imported from 1783–1821.

U.S. exports and imports are not as clearly known and are also not attributed to regions. The U.S. government export reports noted more than 4.5 million fine fur pieces (unspecified) were exported to Canton from the U.S. from 1792–1828. Five to ten thousand bear and 1,000 wolf pelts a year were sent from America to London. A grizzly pelt could be worth up to 150 shillings and a black bear up to 200 shillings. Raccoon fur was popular and almost two million were exported to England in the 1830s, worth 10–30 shillings each. Millions of muskrats were sent even though they were only worth 9¢ each.

The bison became more important as other furs declined. Many people don't realize how far west they once came. The bison could be killed just for the tongue, 25¢; the meat, $2; the hide, $2.50, or simply for sport. William Hornaday (1887) reported that John Fremont mentioned bison in the mountain NW in 1824, "*the buffalo were spread in immense numbers over the Green River and Bear River Valleys, and through all the country lying between the Colorado, or Green River of the Gulf of California, and Lewis' Fork of the Columbia River....*" J. K. Townsend records the occurrence of herds near the Malade, Boise, and Salmon Rivers in 1834. He says the bison frequently moved down both sides of the valley of the Columbia River as far as the Fishing Falls.[34] Around 1834 they began to diminish very rapidly and continued to decrease until 1840.

Fur ships could, and did, turn to whaling. U.S. whaling efforts hit their peak in the mid-1800s as demand for whale oil soared. Sperm oil was the best; baleen, ambergris, and spermaceti were

also in demand. New technologies, including gun-loaded harpoons and steamships, made whalers around the world more efficient. The American whaling fleet, based on the east coast, operated hundreds of ships in the South Atlantic, Pacific, and Indian Oceans. Many species were driven close to extinction. A general moratorium on commercial whaling was finally adopted by the International

Like Steller's Sea Cow the bison almost went extinct.

Whaling Commission in 1982 and took effect in 1986. Japan, Norway, and Iceland are still whaling.

RECAP

The fur trade ebbed and flowed as markets and politics shifted. Ultimately sea otter, fur seal, and beaver harvests collapsed from overhunting. In many areas these key species were virtually wiped out and forgotten.

Market dominance for sea otter furs began with the Russians, then fell to the British, then the Americans. The land fur harvests were dominated by the Russians and British before the American surge of exploration, exploitation, and settlement began.

The advancing wagon trains of eager Americans soon pushed the British to the north and the Russians would sell out of Alaska and retreat. These intense harvests of so many species would have many ecological effects but many remain little studied and largely unknown (more details in Chapter 4).

A Russian koch after sea otters.

CHAPTER 3

Cultural Consequences of the Fur Trade

*T*he quest for furs in the Northwest ultimately involved interactions between Russian, European, and American traders, both heroes and scoundrels, and a complex mix of communities and tribes speaking dozens of languages. Most of these first nations had lived in the region for thousands of years and learned to utilize the available resources with great skill and sophisticated technology. Food and sustenance were sustainably gathered from the far western Aleutians to Baja California and east to the Rocky Mountains.

War, murder and mayhem combined with disease to devastate native communities in the area impacted by the fur trade. Many communities, bands, tribelets, and even tribes were destroyed in less than 50 years. While it was not intentional genocide, in most cases, the results were the same, mirroring the Jewish holocaust, or the Palestinian *Nakba*.[35] More than two-thirds of many tribal populations were gone by the end of this period. In many communities the death toll reached 90% and many simply disappeared. The elimination of these tribes and people made future settlement by Europeans and Americans from California to Alaska much easier.

Cultural differences were often at the root of conflict.[36] Three in particular illustrate the wide gap between the fur traders and the native people. These are first, the intense proprietary nature of some native people; second, the differing attitudes to theft; and third, the nature of war itself. These reflect the environment and the nature of the communities and cultural background of the people involved.

Ownership of resources

Although we might think the native people always freely shared resources (as the misleading fantasy of the Thanksgiving dinner pretends) this was rarely the case. Survival often depended on protecting resources. In the harsh island environment this was particularly important. The Unangan[37] customary law was that no one could collect even driftwood or shellfish in a territory without express permission of the local leadership. Intruders were dealt with swiftly and severely and most often killed.

When the *promyslenniki* arrived they consistently violated these norms and the native people responded. In 1764 four Russian ships were attacked and only four Russians and eight Kamchatkan natives survived; this led to severe reprisals by the Russians. The Unangan fought hard and effectively but were ultimately overcome by firearms, cannon, and organized attacks on isolated populations. Resource conflicts were near universal from the Aleutians to Baja California. Somewhat ironically, theft was not considered as particularly bad in many, if not most, tribal groups.

Thievery

The different understanding of the nature of private property and considerations of theft also led to conflict. The many tribes in the fur world included varied interpretations of theft, but in many cases theft was more of an art form than a crime. As Astorian Ross Cox reported, *"I have seen a fellow stopped on suspicion of stealing an axe. He denied the charge with the most barefaced impudence; and when the stolen article was pulled from under his robe, instead of expressing any regret, he burst out laughing, and alleged he was only joking. One of the (my) men gave him a few kicks, which he endured with great sang froid; and on joining his companions, they received him with smiling countenances, and bantered him on the failure of his attempt."*

Thefts consistently infuriated the European and Russian explorers and traders. Captain James Cook's frustration over a theft led to his death in Hawaii (1779). Many of the worst massacres on both sides could be traced back to a minor theft. These include destruction of the lovely village of Opitsaht (1792); the taking of the *Boston* and killing of all but two of the crew (1803); the killing of a Blackfoot by Meriwether Lewis (1806), the destruction of the *Tonquin* (1811), the gruesome hanging of a native by Astorian John Clarke (1813), the attack on Jedidiah Smith's party on the Umqua (1828), and too many more. In almost every case repercussions would follow leading to a trail of retaliatory destruction for many years. Meriwether Lewis's one deadly shot would result in the death of dozens of innocent trappers years later. Quite often some terrible death or horror would befall an innocent man, party or ship with no knowledge of the past history.

Many furs and other valuable resources were also stolen from the native communities by fur traders. Some of the captains grew angry after native people became more aware of the value of furs and other resources and started asking for more valuable items in trade. In May 1792 for example, Robert Gray ordered an attack on a Chicklisaht Nuu-chah-nulth village north of Nootka Sound and seized the natives' sea otter furs while killing seven. The Chicklisaht took their wounded men to the Spanish outpost at Nootka Sound and asked the commander, Bodega Quadra, to punish Gray. Gray was just one of a number of captains who used force to acquire furs. Often they would take hostages and threaten to kill them unless a fur tribute was paid.

THE NATURE OF WAR

Some territories were stable but not all was peaceful. Trade wars and actual wars and raids were not uncommon and territorial holdings shifted over time. Traditional conflict was often undertaken to collect slaves who were valued and traded across much of the region. Slaves were often taken by force but sometimes purchased. Women and children were most desirable but even the men might be made slaves. Their treatment and opportunities to rise in status varied widely between different tribes.

Although some wars were brutal and devastating, more would end after a few men had been wounded or killed, honorable bravery and courage had been demonstrated, and perhaps some property and resources had been transferred. More severe wars were not unknown and Chief Wickaninnish merged more than ten different nations into the Tla-o-qui-aht and virtually annihilated the Hisau'istahts. Many of the Russians embraced total war, and many of the English and American captains and traders were equally ruthless.

DISEASE

In the 1740s the first[38] foreigners came after land and furs. Deadly diseases were introduced by the early explorers and castaways and increased with the fur traders. The scale of these impacts became clear as the Spanish in the south and Russians to the north stepped up their activity. Although the native families and communities couldn't know it, the crash was coming. The effects can be seen as combining the impact of the Black Death, the Holocaust, and the Palestinian *Nakba*. Within 100 years, 90% of the people in most tribes would be gone and their lands and resources taken. Many tribes and tribelets would simply disappear before being named or studied.

The biggest killer was imported diseases. Native people had little or no resistance to many virulent diseases and an epidemic could easily kill 50–90% of the people infected. Diseases came by sea with sailors and explorers as well as overland from the South and East. Diseases came from Russia, Spain, England, America, Mexico, China, and possibly Japan and the Philippines. Key diseases included: smallpox, dysentery, measles, malaria, mumps, viral influenza, yellow fever, measles, typhoid fever, other fevers (not identified), cholera, and whooping cough (see following table for details). As we have recently relearned, 95% of the people exposed to a person with the measles are likely to be infected.

Even once a scourge had cycled, it could return. Small pox arrived around 1780 in Oregon and would return in 1800–1801, 1824, 1836, 1853, and 1863. Some epidemics were local and others region-wide. In many cases the ship that brought the disease can be identified: the *O'Cain* and respiratory disease to Kodiak (1804), a deadly fever from the galiot *Aleksandr Nevskii* (1802), the intermittent fever of Oregon on the *Owyhee* (1830). In some cases, the natives even identified the person they felt was responsible.

LIST 3.1
Epidemics

Disease	Spread by
Chickenpox	droplet or contact
Cholera	poor sanitation
Common Cold	droplet or contact
Diphtheria	droplet
Dysentery	poor sanitation
Typhus	lice, fleas
Gonorrhea	sexual contact
Influenza	droplet or contact
Malaria	mosquito
Measles	droplet
Mumps	droplet or contact
Whooping cough	droplet
Pneumonia	droplet or contact
Rubella	droplet
Scarlet Fever	droplet or contact
Smallpox	droplet or contact
Syphilis	sexual contact
Tuberculosis	droplet
Typhoid Fever	poor sanitation

VIOLENCE, ACCIDENTS, ABUSE

Violence against the native people was very common as well and led to active resistance in many areas. Soon after the Russians reached Kodiak Island in 1784, Shelikhov's men attacked hundreds of men, women, and children with cannon and musket fire. Only a few people survived by fleeing in *baidarkas*. More than 300 people were killed and when the survivors revisited the place in the summer the stench of the corpses lying on the shore polluted the air so badly that none could stay there.

Many natives also died on otter hunts. As sea otters declined in the Kodiak area and the Aleutians, Baranov required large numbers of Aleuts and Kodiak people to paddle to Sitka in their *baidarkas*, hunting on the way. Parties as large as 600–800 *baidarkas* were

The sea otter fleet

forced to make this perilous journey of over a thousand miles each way. As much as a third of the fleet was lost some years. The ranks of Unangax, Koniag, and Chugach paddlers stayed in close formation to reduce the threat from Tlingit warriors. Some were still killed by the Tlingit, but more were lost at sea.

The paddlers could be surprised by violent storms in crossing the open sea from one promontory to another. They could also be lost to hunger and cold with inadequate food and exhausting long days of paddling. In some cases, the *baidarkas* simply couldn't withstand the stress, and when repairs couldn't be made at sea the paddlers were lost. In 1799 Baranov lost 20 *baidarkas* and 40 men in one storm. On May 2, 1799 a freak wave[39] overtook a party of 60 men and all were lost. In 1799 again, 150 men were poisoned and 115 died from paralytic shellfish poisoning after eating mussels at what is now called Poison

Cove. In 1805 Khlebnikov noted 200 men drowned on the paddle from Kodiak to Sitka and another 100 drowned in other *baidarka* accidents. RAC records show that between 1792 and 1805 more than 750 Koniags (Alutiiq/Sugpiak) were killed in accidents (and this is clearly undercounting).

Many hunters also died after being left on remote islands to hunt. Dropped off with just their *baidarka*, a few tools, and a small amount of food, they were expected to survive and hunt sea otters and other fur-bearing animals. These hunters were left from as far north as the northernmost remote and small Pribilofs to Cedros Island off Baja California. They might be left for years and in some cases they were never picked up. One party was left on a remote northern island for seven years. These abusive practices were one of the factors that led to the taking of the *Tonquin* and the killing of the crew. Twelve Tla-o-qui-aht hunters were left on the Farallon Islands by Captain George Washington Eayers of the *Mercury* and never picked up. Only two managed to survive the 900-mile paddle home.

After they reached their destination they were divided into smaller parties to hunt the intricate inlets where they could be picked off by the Tlingit, Haida, or other tribes. In 1818 in a cooperative project with Baranov, the French Captain Camille de Roquefeuille was compelled to sign an agreement to pay the sum of $200 for any native who might lose his life while in his employ by drowning or at the hands of hostile natives. In the course of his expedition, twenty-six Aleut hunters were killed by the Haidas on Prince of Wales Island, and his fur profits evaporated after he paid for the lost hunters.

The loss of the men to distant hunting and long terms away from home deprived the villages of critical hunters. Old men, women, and children often were required to provide unpaid services, building and repairing *baidarkas*, treating furs, sewing clothes, and other work. This led to further neglect of traditional food collection and preparation and hunger stalked the villages in winter. One observer said the people in one village looked more like corpses than living people and many starved to death throughout the region.

Precontact Aleut population has been estimated at from 8–25,000, but by 1790 it was down 90% to about 2,000. The loss of men in hunting accidents and murder added to the woes. Male/female ratios dropped from roughly 50/50 to 40/60 and as low as 30/70 on Amchitka.

Tribes like the Tlingit that were more warlike and had larger social networks were better able to resist the invasion, but ultimately all lost. In some areas a bounty was offered in later years for killing natives. They were also hunted for sport in parts of California. When they resisted abuse, they were often massacred. In many areas the survivors were relocated to wretched lands, forced to live with former foes,[40] with their children sent away to schools where they were forbidden to speak their native languages.

The impact of these catastrophic losses on families and communities can barely be imagined. Watching your wife, children, parents, and nation fall sick and die when nothing could be done about it would be horrific, as would seeing your husband carried away by the Russians, never to be seen again. The traditional healing practices often made things worse as treatments increased death tolls. The enormous losses contributed to an erosion of faith in the old religions, disruption of social norms, breakdowns in communities, and facilitated the conversion to new religions by the missionaries.

It would be exhausting and depressing to describe all the tragedies of this period so I will focus on just a small subset of tribes that illustrate the scope

CULTURAL CHANGE
ON THE FUR COAST

of the native *Nakba*. The eight tribes I will use as examples are the Unangax (Aleut), Tlingit, Haida, Mowachat (Nootka/Nuu-chah-nulth), Chinook, Seliñ (Interior Salish), Chumash and Nicoleño. The general location of their homelands are shown on the map, while a map of each tribal area is included with the brief description of the tribal history. Boundaries shown are approximate as ownership and use areas shifted under pressure and declines in population.

UNANGAX

At the time of European contact, the Unangax[41,42] inhabited all of the eastern Aleutian Islands, the Alaska Peninsula as far east as Port Moller, and the Shumagin Islands to the south of the Alaska Peninsula. They had lived in the area for at least 7,000 years. The pre-contact population may have been 25,000 or more living in hundreds of villages spread throughout the islands. Because many resources were relatively easy to obtain, all but the youngest and the most elderly or infirm could help acquire food. Despite the harsh conditions, life was good.

The oldest inhabitants of Umnak and Unalaska interviewed said they did not have a tradition of war or conflict, except with the people over an insult to a disabled Unagax from a visiting tribe. Like the Hatfields and McCoys, the two peoples had lived in continual enmity, attacking and plundering each other by turns. The remarks of other early visitors suggest conflicts were more common, but

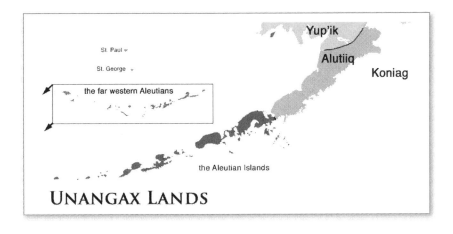

UNANGAX LANDS

Unangan couple

Entrance to Unangan home

the Unangax were ill-prepared to fight the Russians and their guns and cannon.

The first known meeting with Europeans in the North occurred when native paddlers visited Vitus Bering's ship in 1741. Lieutenant Sven Waxell; the biologist Steller; and a Chukchi interpreter who was present to communicate with indigenous peoples and nine other heavily-armed crewmen rowed the longboat to shore. On the beach the Russians encountered men and women, who were *"full of wonder and friendliness."* This pattern of friendly reception was repeated in almost every tribal first contact all the way to California, but it would not last long.

The people referred to themselves as Unangax. Each group was divided into a number of named sub-divisions and the many islands were busy with people. There were two main dialects. An early visitor to The Fox-Islands said the natives were very populous. Unalaska, the largest island, was thought to support several thousand inhabitants. The Unangax lived

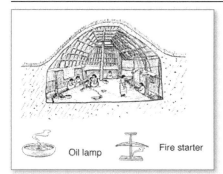

Oil lamp   Fire starter

Aleut ulax, ulaq Sugpiaq ciqlluaq, Russian Barabara.

in communities composed of fifty (and sometimes of two or even three hundred) people. They lived in large earth-sheltered wooden structures called *barabaras* up to 120–240 feet long, from 18–24 feet wide, and 12–15 feet high. Several openings were made in the top of the larger complexes and inhabitants went in and out by ladders. The smallest dwellings might have just two or three entrances of this sort while the largest five or more. Each structure was divided into alcoves and by partitions for families. These might be marked by means of stakes driven into the earth.

The Unangax neighbors included the Sugpiaq[43] speakers on the coast from Kupreanof Point to Cook's Inlet and Kodiak Island.[44] The Dena'ina Athabaskan Indians were to the east, an inland people

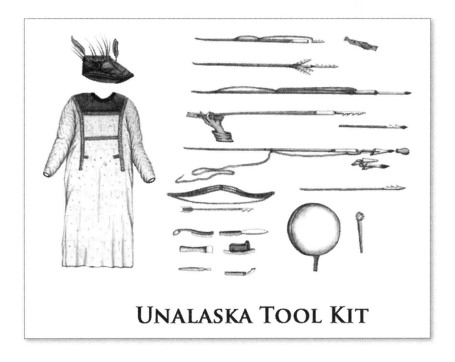

UNALASKA TOOL KIT

who had moved into the region around 1,000 years earlier; and finally, the Yup'ik speakers to the northeast. Conflicts between tribes occurred and slaves were captured and traded. The slaves could be prisoners of war taken in raids on other villages or purchased. Some slaves became wives, and children might be adopted. Some were integrated into the community while others remained in slave status and might be sacrificed in tributes or ceremonies.

The *promyshlenniki* fur hunters and traders used brutality, terror, force and firearms to make the Unangax and their neighbors hunt for sea otters, fur seals, and other desirable game. The treatment of natives was appalling even for that time in history, and included murder, sexual exploitation, and mayhem of all kinds. Unangax fought back against Russian intrusion and prevented them from establishing permanent hunting camps for many years.

In 1761 the men of the Russian ship *Sv. Gravil* committed unspeakable and unprovoked atrocities on the Unangax. In December 1763, the Unangax overcame long-time ethnic disagreements with the Alutiiq and mounted a joint counter attack. The Russians lost four vessels and only twelve out of two hundred men survived. In 1766, Russian avengers killed many hundreds of Unangax. The Russian leader Ivan Solov'ev vowed to reduce the population from 25,000 to 2,500 and his men systematically killed men and enslaved the women and children. The Russian Orthodox bishop, Innokentii Veniaminov, reported that Solov'ev murdered about 3,000 Unangax. On one island Solov'ev landed on the shore and exterminated all the Unangax who were there with their wives and children. The sea around the islet became bloody from the bodies thrown into it. He also systematically destroyed their weapons, *baidarkas*, and larger skin boats resulting in death by starvation.

When Empress Catherine the Great took the throne in 1762, she hoped to inspire a liberal European way of approaching governance and improving treatment of all people. She attempted to reform the tribute system by abolishing the use of hostages and terminating quotas for pelts. To prevent the destruction of native cultures she also proclaimed a policy of isolation and ordered the Orthodox Church to set up churches, schools, and charity programs in Siberia that would then be extended to Russian America. The church did make some effort to help the workers and natives as we see from Hiero Monk Makarii's Letter to St Petersburg, "*The Shelikhov and Golikov company men threaten other people in a most barbarous way. They lack any human kindness. They take their wives and daughters as mistresses by force, they kill the people. They send out the men to hunt sea otter from the earliest spring, healthy or ailing, it does not matter. Some of those who are ill, die en route. They keep the men hunting until fall and there is no time to put up food for themselves and their families, nor get materials for clothing. They starve to death and suffer from cold because of lack of clothing. When they are subjected to severe floggings, they commit suicide. If an Aleut does not bring in plenty of fox pelts, they strip him and pin him to the ground and beat him with sinew cords, all the time chanting that 'we do not tolerate laziness.'*"

Sadly, her liberal impulses were faintly felt in Alaska because, "*God dwells on high, and the Empress is very far away.*" The violence against natives continued as the Russians moved east. Over the next several years, Shelikhov's men continued to coerce more people to work and any show of rebellion was thwarted by deploying weapons, instilling terror, and hostage-taking.

In discussion with natives many years later Fr. Veniaminov found that Petr Natrubin had seen relations deteriorate with the Aleuts on Avatanak as the Russians abused the natives and gathered resources without permission. The natives finally took action and attacked Natrubin and his men, but the attack failed. In retribution Natrubin killed many people on Avatanak and after Natrubin's crew crossed over to Tigalda Island the Aleuts took refuge on a small rock pillar off-shore. With its vertical walls and flat, grass-covered top, the rock had always offered protection from marauders, but the Aleuts were fully exposed to the fire from the rifles carried by the hunters and the Aleuts were all shot down. These were not isolated cases and after discussions with the Unangax Fr. Veniaminov estimated as many as 5,000 Unangax had been murdered. The *promyshlenniki* couldn't kill them all because they relied on the Unangax for their hunting, boating and survival skills.

The Unangax treatment under the Russian America Company (RAC) after 1800 was only slightly better. It was strongly influenced by the nature of serfdom in Russia, where serfs were only slightly better off than slaves, with few rights or opportunities. Under the new charter the Unangax were to receive no pay; but this led to poor hunting results and before long payment for furs resumed. The RAC also forbade Unangax to sell furs or meats to visiting ships but this was hard to enforce. They also at times restricted subsistence fishing to the shores of their villages and prohibited them from leaving their villages without official permission.

At times half of the Unangax men were mandated to serve as hunters (sometimes four out of five men were required to go) for as long as three or four years at a time. This demand was enforced with threats, even after the RAC took over. In 1801 the monks reported that the RAC overseers drove the men on an otter hunting party by preparing leg irons and neck yokes, laying out birch switches to whip young ones, ropes to whip the thirty-year-olds with, and canes for the old men. After coming ashore, the Russian hunters aimed their loaded rifles and said, *"If you don't want to go on the expedition, just say so now (cocking their guns) and we'll shoot!" One man began to protest so they put him in irons and flogged him until he was hoarse from screaming and could hardly say, 'Yes—I'll go.'"* To reduce resistance every chief had to surrender his children as hostages. Additional hunters could also be forced to hunt by hostage-taking. In 1790, one company reportedly held 300 hostages, including 200 daughters of leaders, subject to sexual abuse.

There were exceptions to the inhumane treatment and slaughter of Unangax. Some of the Russian managers and workers developed good working relations and friendships with the Unangax. Some married Unangax women and took them home to Russia after their service was completed. Eventually some of the Unangax became salaried workers on ships and in camps and worked for the RAC for many years.

Fatalities occurred from conflicts involving armed alliances between the *promyshlenniki* and the Unangax. The Russians exploited existing local conflicts and Unangax also used their Russian allies in efforts to settle old scores. For example, in the late 1760s the Russian Afanasii Ocheredin allied with the people of Umnak Island against the Four Mountains' islanders. Russian captains united with Fox Islands warriors in a war with the Alutiiq in the 1770s. Even later many native tribes working with the RAC participated in Baranov's armed encounters with the Tlingit. Anywhere from 40 to over 200 Unangax were killed during the Sitka wars. A large group of Unangax *baidarkas* towed the warship *Neva* into position to fire its cannons at the Tlingit fort when Sitka was retaken.

The increased stress, reduced food, and exposure to European diseases were deadly. A series of epidemics swept through the islands, along the coast, and on the Alaskan peninsula, beginning before 1800. More catastrophic episodes included a deadly fever from Russia in 1802, a respiratory disease in 1804 and a worse recurrence in 1806–1807 with *"not enough people left to bury the dead."* In 1807 dysentery struck, followed by the flu and measles in 1819, again in 1827–28. Respiratory disease retuned in 1830, with typhoid in a very deadly epidemic in 1832. The small pox returned in 1835–40, followed by the flu in 1836 and the measles in 1848. Some of these were local while others widespread. Mortality was often quite high; above 50% in some years. Within 50 years of contact the Unangax population had been reduced by 80%. In 1834 only twenty-seven villages remained. By 1800 the population had dropped to 2,500 and would fall further by the turn of the century when the "Great Sickness," a combination of flu and measles, devastated the region yet again. Only 499 Unangax were counted in 1906, and yet more sorrow and population loss was to come with the 1918 small pox and flu.

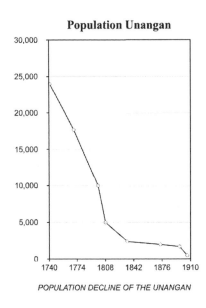

Population Unangan

POPULATION DECLINE OF THE UNANGAN

The decline had been caused by the murder, abuse and mistreatment of the people; conflict between Unangax and Russians; introduced diseases; the hazards of long-distance enforced hunting; and starvation from communities that had lost their hunters and hunting gear. The RAC forcibly resettled many Unangax in work groups[45] at or near the sources of furs and this led to further disruption of families and communities. Some survivors were also enslaved, with some women held as slaves as late as 1900, more than 35 years after the Emancipation Proclamation.

The Unangax would face another great challenge in World War II. The Japanese forces that attacked Unalaska (Iliuliuk) in 1942 took 44 of them to horrific prison camps in Japan where half died. Villages, equipment, and houses on some islands were burned by the U.S. forces to make it harder for Japanese invaders. Almost 900 Unangax were rounded up by the U.S. military after being given 24 hours to pack a suitcase and close up their homes. They were shipped to SE Alaska and placed in abandoned fish canneries. Inadequate housing, appalling food, and a lack of medical care led to many hardships. As Philemon M. Tutiakoff recounted, *"The overcrowded conditions were an abomination. There were 28 of us forced to live in one, designated 15'x20' house. There existed no church, no school, no medical facility, no store, no community facility, no skiffs or dories, no fishing gear and no hunting rifles."* Thirty-two died at the Funter Bay camp, seventeen at Killisnoo, twenty at Ward Lake, five at Burnett Inlet. Yet despite their poor treatment at the hands of the U.S. government, twenty-five Unangax̂ men joined the Armed Forces. Three took part in the U.S. invasion to reclaim Attu Island, and all were awarded the Bronze Star.

All were affected by this appalling treatment. When they returned to the north they were simply dropped off. They found their homes had been ransacked and despoiled by soldiers, and their boats, sleds, rifles and equipment were damaged or missing. Their dog teams had also been lost. The residents of Attu were not allowed to return home because it would "cost too much." Yet, against all odds, the Unangax have survived and still live in the region.

Today there are about 2,000 Unangan and more than 100 people who still speak the native language. There is an online course to help teach the language: https:// unangan.community.uaf.edu/ introduction/.

THE TLINGIT

The Tlingit[46] lived on the southeastern coast and among the islands of Alaska for 11,000 years. At the time of contact they were a prosperous and powerful tribe, united by language and custom; but were not a political *nation.* Pre-contact population may have been as high as 40,000 with more than twenty tribes in the Tlingit world. Most villages were on the shoreline but there were also several closely related inland tribelets. The Nass River appears to have been a center of development for the Tlingit. A village might include 1,000 people or more. Matrilineal clans were particularly important. Society, arts, and religion were highly developed. The Tlingit sea-going canoes travelled hundreds of miles for trade or raids.

The complex island, sea, waterways, rivers, and forests provided excellent resources for sustenance, housing and crafts. This allowed time for refined arts and crafts. In many areas the Tlingit

A Tlingit Village

village would make a seasonal round between winter, summer and fall settlements following the availability of fish, mammals, berries and other resources. Winter villages included very large and comfortable homes made of giant wooden planks. Some Tlingit groups specialized in marine mammal hunts.

Although clans might raid and fight with each other, the Tlingit also formed alliances in the face of common enemies. Wars and raiding parties were also carried out in cooperation with other tribal

Tlingit with Bear Cub

Tlingit armor was effective

Tlingit chief

groups. In the early 1800s the Tlingit allied with the Kaigani and other Haida tribes to make a big slave raid south to Puget Sound. Captives were enslaved and traded.

The Tlingit probably met foreigners for the first time before 1741. In that year, perhaps as a result of previous but undocumented ill treatment or disease introduction, they attacked Alexei Chirikov's expedition and took two boats. In 1774, Juan Josef Pérez Hernández had much more pleasant interactions with the Tlingit and drawings from his expedition provide invaluable records of Tlingit life. In 1775, Spanish explorer Bruno de Hezeta accidentally introduced small pox to the Tlingit with deadly consequences. Captain Nathaniel Portlock talked with an older man in 1789 who had lost ten children to the small pox. He noted, "*I expected to have seen a numerous tribe, and was quite surprised when I found that it consisted only of three men, three women, the same number of girls, two boys about twelve years old, and two infants... The old man endeavored to describe the excessive torments he endured whilst he was afflicted with the disorder that had marked his face and gave me to understand that happened some years ago. This convinced me that they had had the small-pox among them at some distant period. He told me that the distemper carried off great numbers of the inhabitants, and that he himself had lost ten children by it."*

Captain James Cook arrived in 1778 and the sea otter fur ships arrived in the mid-1780s. In 1791 Spanish explorer Alessandro Malaspina met with the Tlingit at Yakutat Bay. Malaspina's scholars made the first serious study of the tribe. Other explorers and fur traders contacted the Tlingit before Alexander Baranov established Sitka in 1799.

Tlingit Princess

The Russian treatment of the Tlingit was not good, so a coalition of villages attacked and took the fort at Sitka in 1802. They built a fort of their own, complete with cannons. In 1804, after a large but indecisive battle that included the Russian warship *Neva,* the Tlingit retreated[47] and the Russians retook Sitka, rebuilt the fort and community. In 1808, Sitka became the headquarters for the RAC in Alaska. The Tlingit would not return to live in Sitka until 1824. Tlingit resistance continued throughout the occupation, with isolated parties of Russians and their hunters always at risk of attack.

The Tlingit had long established trading routes and connections with the interior and other tribes. They took full advantage of these in dealing with the European traders. They held off the Russians for many years but traded with them. Their strength enabled them to receive prices for their furs that were three times higher than the Unangax and Koniag hunters.

A Russian observer noted in 1835, that, *"This people—populous, powerful, daring, and, having an inclination toward barter and trade— are industrious and diligent. They ably adopt European customs and, with innate cleverness and intelligence, become quickly adapted to firearms."* The Tlingit intercepted, managed, and profited as middlemen from fur movement from the inland areas for sale to the foreigners. First they worked with the Russians, then British and American ships, and finally through the Hudson's Bay Company posts and ships.

Tlingit society was better able than most to resist and survive the onslaught of the Russians and Europeans. The tribe was large and well-dispersed. Strong clans and communities helped in the face of disease and conflict.

From an original population of perhaps 40,000 the Tlingit dropped to 25–30,000 in 1806 as a result of disease and conflict. The fall continued to 10,000 in 1835 and down to 6,000 in 1840 after a new and deadly round of small pox.

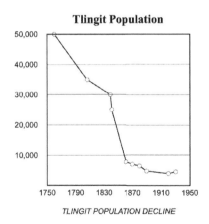

TLINGIT POPULATION DECLINE

This ongoing catastrophe encouraged conversion to the new religion. The Tlingit continue to live in the area and have maintained much of their culture despite the onslaught. The University of Alaska Southeast offers a minor in Tlingit Language. Yukon College offers a Tlingit course as well. Several lower grades offer introductions to the language and initiatives to start a Tlingit language immersion program are underway.

HAIDA LANDS

Young Haida Woman

HAIDA

Archaeological evidence confirms continual habitation on the Haida Islands for at least 6,000 years. At first contact, 15,000 people probably lived in the 126 known villages in the area, and it is likely the total might have been 20–30,000 before contact. The original Haida family structure divided the members into two groups, the Raven and the Eagle. These groups were further divided into many clans. Individuals proclaimed clan membership through an elaborate display of inherited family crests carved on totem poles. The society is matrilineal with property, titles, names, crests, masks, performances, and even songs passed from one generation to the next, through the mother's side.

The Haida were feared along the coast for their lightning raids against their enemies. They rapidly replaced the bows, arrows and short spears with firearms when they became available. They also added cannons to their village defenses. Their great skills of seamanship, superior great canoes (later with mounted cannons) and

Haida Village

Haida warrior with flint lock musket

Haida chief

their island fortress added to the aggressive posture of the Haida towards neighboring tribes.

First contact may have been in 1774, with the Spanish explorer Juan Pérez. In 1787, British Captain George Dixon initiated trade with the Haida for sea otter skins. The Haida adapted and survived. The lip disk fell from favor. For the next fifty years, the Haida traded sea otter pelts with European trading ships for guns, iron, manufactured goods, and potatoes, which the Haida then began to cultivate themselves.

When George Vancouver first came to the Strait of Georgia in 1793, he found that a smallpox epidemic in 1782 had littered the area with corpses. Skulls were strewn about abandoned, overgrown villages; whole sections of coastline were strewn with skulls, limbs, ribs and backbones in great numbers.

In August 1793, a skirmish broke out between boats from the *Discovery* and the Haida when the seemingly friendly natives tried to seize British guns and ammunition. Natives hurled spears from their canoes and

Vancouver ordered his men to fire. Volleys from the ship sent the attackers to shore where they abandoned their canoes and ran off into the woods, leaving several dead behind.

A Kaiganee Haida chief in 1845 was asked if he would like to go to America or England. He emphatically declined the offer because he considered everyone slaves—even the captains, who were always at work. He spoke English well and said, *"I have slaves who hunt for me— paddle me in my canoes, and my wives to attend upon me. Why should I wish to leave?"*

In 1834 the Hudson's Bay Company established Fort Simpson as a trading post in Tsimshian territory and this became the center of trade. This disrupted the traditional economy and led the Haida to conflict with the Kwakiutl. The new traders also brought a catastrophic smallpox epidemic to the Queen Charlotte Islands. The population dropped dramatically with the arrival of European diseases and by 1911 only 589 native people lived in Old Masset and Skidegate. Only 2–3% of the original population remained.

So much knowledge and wisdom was lost, but the Haida have maintained much of their culture. Today the 2,500 Haida still enjoy the traditional foods of salmon, halibut, herring roe on kelp, and seaweed. Another 2,000 Haida live outside the area.

The tribal members have played a crucial role in efforts to save the Haida-Gwaii ecosystem from commercial logging and development. The turning point came in the winter of 1985–86 when the Haida elders blocked logging trucks near the village of Hlk'yah GawGa on Lyell Island. The Xaad Kihlgaa Hl Suu.u Society strives to preserve the Haida language. The Society assists the Xaad Kil Gwaaygangee (language nest), school programs, the Simon Fraser University Haida language proficiency program, and the Skidegate and Alaska language groups as well.

MOWACHAHT (NOOTKA)
The Mowachaht are one of the tribes that have often been called the Nootka[48] people. The Nootka had a ranked society, divided into

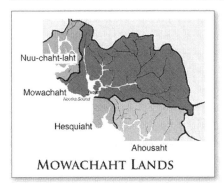

MOWACHAHT LANDS

the nobility, the commoners, and slaves. The Nootka were hunter-gatherers who made their living primarily from the sea. Fish (particularly salmon and halibut), sea mammals, and shellfish were mainstays. One of the key villages was Yuquot on Friendly Sound.

Pre-contact population for the Nootka was possibly as high as 50,000 in 25 known tribes. Epidemics and conflict would lead to a 90% drop in population by 1900. Smallpox and other impacts of contact resulted in the disappearance of many groups and the absorption of others into neighboring groups before the Russians and Europeans arrived. When James Cook first encountered the villagers at Yuquot in 1778, one story suggests they directed him to "come around" (Nuu-chah-nulth nuutkaa) to bring his ship around the point into a protected harbor. Cook thought they were telling him their name. Cook's sailors traded sea otter pelts with the Nootka, and his crew found out later that they could be sold at a great profit in China. This triggered the European rush into the maritime fur trade.

Yuquot village, also known as Nootka and Friendly Cove, soon became a major trading center. Chief Maquinna and his village controlled much of the trade at and around Nootka Sound.

The Mowachat town of Yuquot

Mowachat Women in Large Wooden Lodge

In pre-contact days, 500+ people occupied the village of Yuquot. Jewitt describes the village as having about 20 houses built in a line, facing the cove: *"They vary not much in width, being usually from 36 to 40 feet wide, but are of very different lengths. That of the king, which is much the longest being about 150 feet, while the smallest, which contained only 2 families, do not exceed 40 feet in length."* The houses were constructed with a frame of permanent posts and beams made from thick cedar logs. The siding and roofing were wide cedar planks that traveled with the people on the yearly round.

During the spring and summer, the Mowachaht lived on the coast at Yuquot. Sea food, whales and fish were eaten. In early September the villagers removed the wide cedar planks from the house frames, stacked them on large canoes, and moved about 20 miles up the sound to Tahsis.

Here the boards were placed on the house frames and the village began to harvest the salmon run from the river, hunt bears and deer in the nearby mountains, and collect berries. For the next two months the salmon were cured for winter's provisions. Salmon

Trading session at Nootka Bay

eggs were collected in great tubs. Salal berries were collected and pressed into large cakes.

At the end of December, the village moved to Coopte. Here the harvest of herring and sprat began, with some salmon. There was nothing but feasting from morning till night according to Jewitt. They then returned to Yuquot in late February.

Juan Jose Peréz Hernandez may have been the first to reach Nootka in 1774. In August, his crew traded with the Mowachaht, offering Californian abalone shells. The Spanish did not stay long but apparently did bring small pox to Nootka. By 1791 John Boit and John Hoskins (*Columbia*) noted its presence and the natives claimed the Spanish brought it. Explorers accounts of other tribes mention abandoned villages with skulls scattered about in 1792.

British Captain James Hanna in the 60-ton brig *Sea Otter* arrived in 1785. Hanna punished some of the "savages" by firing on them for the theft of a chisel. As the chief Maquinna later reported to Spanish Captain Esteban Martinez, "*... a capt. Hannah much offended the natives. One of them had been on board his ship and stole from him a carpenter's chisel. The next day there being a number of canoes lying* *along side the ship the captain fired upon them and killed men, women and children to the number of twenty. The chief being on board jumped from the quarter deck and swam ashore…"*

Captain Martinez added that, *"He (Hannah) went among the villages situated along the NE arm of the inlet, where he killed more than fifty Indians."* To further inflame feelings, when Maquinna visited the ship later, gunpowder was spread under his chair. They pretended this was an honor the British showed to chiefs. Maquinna thought it was dark-colored sand but when one of crew set off the charge the chief was raised from the deck, his buttocks burned. He later showed Captain Martinez the scars.

In June 1791, John Boit and John Hoskins of the ship *Columbia* noted the presence at Nitinaht village of smallpox (brought by the Spaniards the natives said) and venereal disease. Jose Mariano Mozino, a doctor and naturalist at Nootka Sound in 1792 already noted the impact of venereal disease. *"This wantoness has surely been sad for those small settlements, which are gradually weakened by the ravages of venereal disease; within a few years it can ruin them so that the entire race will perish. These, sterilized by this pernicious contagion, ought to fear the unfortunate fate of the people of Baja California, of whose race there scarcely remains one or two, the rest consumed by the raging syphilis which the sailors of our ships have spread among them."*

Chief Maquinna and his wives

From 1789–1794, the tribes were involved in the Nootka Sound Controversy, a bitter dispute between the Spanish and British over control of the area. Chief Maquinna took advantage of the popularity of Nootka Sound to manipulate relations between the disputing nations. In 1789 Esteban José Martínez was sent to occupy Nootka Sound and validate Spanish sovereignty. Arriving on May 5, they quickly built a small fort. Several British and American ships were also working in the area. British Captain James Colnett[49] of the *Argonaut* had brought building materials and a Chinese labor force to build a trading post on land previously "purchased" from the local tribe by John Meares. The Spanish arrested Colnett and seized several ships and crews. The captured Chinese were put to work building the Spanish Fort San Miguel. At the end of the summer when Martínez headed south, the American ships and crews were released, but the British ships and crews were taken to San Blas. Colnett and his crew were ultimately released and returned to the NW coast. This could have led to war, but both countries had other problems to deal with at the time.

In 1790 Francisco de Eliza y Reventa arrived at Yuquot and began to build a small settlement. After the Spaniards plundered a local village for planks to build their structures, tensions rose but Maquinna was later reassured, and in October he helped search for survivors of a shipwreck. The quarrel between European nations was eventually settled by negotiation that led to the Nootka Conventions. In 1792 Juan Francisco de la Bodega Quadra arrived at Yuquot to arrange implementation of the terms. Maquinna struck up a close relationship with him and was his frequent dinner guest. Bodega became convinced, partly by Maquinna's testimony, that Meares's land claim was unfounded, and when George Vancouver arrived in August to repossess Meares's land, Maquinna found himself feted by both sides. He proved adept in the art of diplomacy and entertaining the foreign emissaries at the village of Tahsis. When Bodega left Nootka Sound in September, Yuquot was still in Spanish hands. The competition between Spain and the Great Britain for Nootka

Sound was eventually settled with the Nootka Conventions of the 1790s, with Spain agreeing to abandon claims to the North Pacific coast. In March 1795 the Europeans finally left and the Mowachaht tore down the buildings, reclaimed their planks, and reasserted their ownership.

Mowachat with bow and quiver

By the mid-1790s, the sea otter population was depleted and trade was declining. The economic hardships that followed may have led the the younger Maquinna (1796–1825) to capture the trading ship *Boston* in 1803. When the *Boston* arrived at Nootka Sound in March 1803, the chiefs of the Mowachaht had been trading with Europeans for more than two decades. He greeted the new arrival as was customary, coming aboard to welcome the captain and assess the trading possibilities. He offered Captain John Salter fresh salmon as a welcome gesture and later received a gift—a double-barreled musket with which he shot some ducks and made a gift of them to Salter in the ongoing escalation of business protocol.

In the course of the hunt, one of the locks on the gun had broken and Maquinna told Salter that it was *peshak*, that it was bad. Salter assumed the chief had broken it with misuse and called him a liar (among other insults), and worse yet, struck Maquinna on the head with the breach of the musket. Maquinna knew some English, and Jewitt could see that Maquinna understood Captain Salter's insults all too well. He said not a word in reply but his countenance sufficiently expressed the rage he felt. The news spread through the village of the high affront to their chief and other chiefs, sub-chiefs, and warriors assembled on a nearby beach. Maquinna sat silent and attentive as an orator set forth the case against Captain Salter, reminding them of their kin who had been slain by Captain Hanna.

On March 22, 1803, warriors from the village of Yuquot attacked and took the *Boston*. The Mowachaht warriors killed all but two members of the twenty-six-man crew. Having the ship completely in their possession, without the loss of a man, Maquinna ordered the cable cut. They set the fore top sail and had Jewitt steer the ship to Friendly Cove. Here they hauled her onto the beach and began to unload the cargo.

The ill treatment of natives was very common and led to subsequent revenge attacks in many areas. Often these fell on innocent and well-behaved ships or traders. In 1811, the Tla-o-qui-aht band attacked and destroyed the trading ship *Tonquin* in Clayoquot Sound as an act of revenge for similar mistreatment.

The Nootka people were innovators and quickly adopted the potato. The Ozette-Nootka potato is likely the descendent of a potato planted in Nootka Bay as early as 1791. This species has been kept for more than 200 years by generations of native gardeners. Unlike most other potatoes grown in North America today, which arrived from potatoes grown in Europe, the Ozette Nootka was brought directly from South America by the Spanish. It is a promising potato for wider use today.

The Mowachaht and Muchalaht formally combined in the 1950s and currently have more than 600 members. The Mowachaht/Muchalaht First Nations have opened up the Yuquot Historic Village site for visitors from around the world. Since 1923 Yuquot has been a National Historic Site of Canada and the tribes have applied for World Heritage recognition.

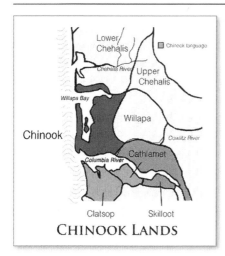

CHINOOK LANDS

Chief Comcomly

CHINOOK

The first visitors to the Chinook noted their work ethic, trading ability, good sense and intelligence.[50] They made a yearly round of summer and winter villages in a resource-rich environment they had occupied for more than ten thousand years. The summer villages were on the Columbia River while the winter villages were on protected Willapa Bay. At the time of Lewis and Clark, the most important Chinook village was Qwatsa'mts at the mouth of the Chinook River on Baker's Bay. This plank-house settlement was home to the powerful one-eyed chief Comcomly. Lewis and Clark estimated there were 28 houses with about 400 residents. The Chinook flattened the heads of their babies and looked with some contempt upon "round heads." Clark was frustrated by their skills as traders, honed over generations of intertribal trade. He complained that, *"they are never satisfied for what they receive in return is ten times the value of the articles they gave."*

Chinook Plank Lodge

Their exceptional skills in boats were also noted by many visitors, including Lewis and Clark and John Jacob Astor's men. Their wooden canoes were simple but well-shaped. Some were 40 feet long, six feet wide, and able to carry 30 people. While Lewis and Clark's men huddled in their damp leather clothing in their dark and dank quarters and cursed the foul weather, the Chinooks went about their daily routine and defied the worst waves and winds in their canoes wearing hats and capes admirably suited to wet days. Clark noted, *"Certain it is they are the best canoe navigators I ever saw,"* as he watched them paddling comfortably in huge stormy seas.

Variants of the Chinook language were spoken by many of the nations from the mouth of the Columbia to the falls. The importance of their trading led to a hybrid language known as the Chinook jargon[51] that became the language of maritime and river traders. The wealth and status of chiefs along the Lower Columbia in the early years of the fur trade was elevated by the HBC policy of seeking to organize the fur trade by selecting leaders to work with. Wealth along the Columbia River was soon consolidated by a small number of chiefs, who ascended to newly elevated roles in the region.

Chief Comcomly became regionally dominant in a way that would have been difficult to achieve even a generation before. He became one of the principal chiefs of the confederacy of all the Chinook tribes along the Columbia between the Cascade Range and the sea (except the Clatsops). He had wives from many of the tribes within the confederacy. To provide support for his large family he also had many slaves. Peter Corney described him as *"a short elderly man— the richest and most powerful chief on the River."* David Thompson in 1811 found him *"a strong, well-made man, his hair short,*

of dark brown, and naked except a short kilt around his waist to the middle of the thigh." (For more see Comcomly bio in Book 2, Tenacity.)

George Simpson noted, *"The Chinooks (are) keen traders and through their hands nearly the whole of our Furs pass, indeed so tenacious are they of this Monopoly that their jealousy would carry them the length of pillaging or even murdering strangers who come to the*

Chinook Woman and Child

Establishment if we did not protect them." Comcomly's understanding of the traders and his many slaves and family connections gave the Chinooks an advantage in the movement of goods and interactions with customers.

In 1805 the Chinooks told Lewis and Clark of deadly small pox outbreaks in 1776[52] and 1801. Lewis and Clark also counted many cases of gonorrhea and syphilis for which there was no good treatment. Other diseases had also taken their toll and many villages had been depopulated by 1800. The population distribution in different clans is not known, but perhaps only 500 people were under Comcomly when Lewis and Clark arrived. His influence grew rapidly and he was able to generously offer 800 warriors to help the Americans fight the British during the War of 1812. He retired in 1824 and transferred his name and chieftainship to his son Shalapau.

Already ravaged by other diseases when the HBC did a population count in 1824–25, the Chinooks under Comcomly had declined to 720, including slaves. By late 1825 Chief Comcomly had lost *"eight individuals of his family to disease."* This was apparently the measles. The Chinooks vacated their village at Point Ellis as a result of the horror of so many deaths. Two of his favorite sons, Chalakan and Choulits, were gone. Worse was soon to come as the intermittent fever arrived on the *Owyhee* under Captain John Dominis. This new fever was catastrophic. Comcomly and many of the Chinook people died of the fever. Francis Ermatinger reported it was common to see bodies floating by in the Columbia River. Many villages were abandoned and later burned by Hudson's Bay Company employees to dispose of the bodies.

Many families and tribes disappeared completely, *"many others* (tribes) *have been swept off entirely by this fatal disease, without leaving a single survivor to tell their melancholy tale."* Thousands died and as people fled the epidemic they helped spread it. HBC Chief Factor John McLoughlin estimated that nine-tenths of the native population were swept away by these epidemics. From 1831–1839 the disease was carried around the Northwest and to California by fur traders and native travelers. Most Europeans were sickened but eventually recovered thanks to quinine, better treatment, and innate resistance; but mortality ranged from 60–90% or higher in the native population.

In 1836, small pox returned. Very rough estimates of the population in eleven of the Chinook-speaking tribes suggested a population of more than 20,000 in 1780, but by 1805 the number was reduced to about 12,000. When Lt. Charles Wilkes of the U.S. Exploring Expedition visited the region in 1841, he counted just 575 Chinook survivors on the Columbia River. There were so few Chinooks left, even including people from other tribes and groups who had joined them, that the tribe was not recognized by the federal government. This travesty should be addressed and the Chinook should be recognized as a tribe, and allocated land.

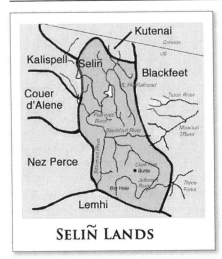

SELIÑ LANDS

SELIÑ

The Seliñ[53] refer to themselves as Sqélio̐—the People. The original territory of the Seliñ extended from the crest of the Bitterroot Range to the Continental Divide of the Rocky Mountains, centered on the upper reaches of the Clark Fork of the Columbia River. Before contact there were several bands based east of the Continental Divide, as far east and south as the Big Hole Valley (near today's Butte and Helena) and the Three Forks of the Missouri. The pre-contact population may have been 20,000 or more but it is really not known or knowable.

The Plateau region between the Rocky Mountains and the coastal mountains is semiarid with sagebrush, grass, and pine groves interwoven with plentiful rivers and streams that once provided plentiful salmon and other fish to the people. Deer, elk, bison and other big game helped ensure a reliable food supply. Most

Seliñ woman

Seliñ tribes were divided into autonomous, loosely organized bands of related families, each with its own chief and local territory. In winter a band would occupy a river village; in summer it would travel, living at campsites that provided good hunting, fishing, and gathering of wild plant foods.

The Seliñ followed these seasons in closely-knit families and tribes, sharing the joys of family life. Dances, music,

Seliñ man

games, and all-important storytelling enriched their lives. Their way of life was part of an inter-tribal system with an extensive network of exchange. They believed then, and now, that all things, humans, animals, plants, rocks, and soil are interconnected.

Relations with neighboring tribes varied over time and were mostly cordial. However, to the East, conflicts with the Blackfeet, Gros Ventre, and others occurred. Intertribal warfare was generally ceremonial in nature with relatively low casualty rates. Counting coup[54] on the enemy was the most important aspect of warfare. Women and children were taken to be sold or used as slaves.

After horses reached the area around 1730, the culture of the Seliñ changed. They could now mount annual fall expeditions to hunt bison on the plains. The acquisition of horses increased mobility and conflict, particularly with the Blackfeet. The community began to emphasize plains-type warfare and its honors. The Blackfeet obtained firearms from traders first and that enabled them to harass the Seliñ and discourage traders from crossing the Rockies. However, trade still occurred between these enemies when formal truces were arranged.

By the 1790s the Seliñ had managed to obtain a few firearms through intertribal trade and were better able to defend themselves. As trading increased they were able to get even more firearms. They journeyed as far east as the Mandan villages to get them. Seliñ people were seen there by trader Alexander Henry the Younger in 1806 at one of the great trade fairs. By 1810, NWC traders managed to work around the Blackfeet to supply arms to the Seliñ.

On September 4, 1805, the band Lewis and Clark met in the upper Bitterroot Valley included 440 people pasturing 500 horses. They were preparing for the fall bison hunt and harvesting choke cherries when Lewis and Clark arrived. They were able to buy eleven horses and exchange seven others. The chief was hospitable and they smoked the peace pipe. Lewis and Clark found the language unique and had difficulty communicating with the Seliñ, going through multiple language translations. The Seliñ met the strangers with hospitality and vital provisions but received little in return. This was to be the story of their relations with the whites. Few tribes were as peaceful, cooperative, and friendly as the Seliñ but in the end it did little to stop their mistreatment.

Smallpox killed as many as half of the Seliñ about 1780. After traders started to arrive in greater numbers new diseases struck. Epidemics of influenza, measles, and other contagious diseases hit hard. Smallpox struck again in 1825, the intermittent fever reached the area in the 1830s, and there were repeated bouts of influenza throughout the 1830s.

Pressure from settlers and trappers was pushing many tribes to the West and as they entered occupied territory this increased

Seliñ village

conflicts over food and other resources. The Seliñ were eventually pushed out of their eastern territory but still returned to the East for buffalo hunts for many years. The European trappers, traders, and settlers also brought new access to guns and alcohol and this contributed to greater violence. The fur trade spread rapidly in the early 1800s.

From 1807–1809, Jocko Finlay, a free trapper, and his family were residing with the Seliñ. In 1809 David Thompson established Saleesh House near present day Thompson Falls, Montana. This NWC post facilitated trade with the Seliñ. David Thompson noted that, *"they were a fine race of moral Indians, the finest I had seen."* Saleesh House was well placed in a beaver-rich area and operated for many decades. In 1810 Thompson and other members of the NWC linked Saleesh House with Spokane House by improving a trail known as the Skeetshoo Indian Road. In 1811, Joseph Beaulieu was a free trader in the area around Saleesh House. Joseph Howse from the HBC built and occupied a competing trading post called Howse House from 1810 to 1811. The HBC took over Saleesh House after the merger in 1821 and may have operated the post until about 1850. The HBC also opened Fort Colville, located near Kettle Falls, in 1825. This post on the Columbia River was within reach as it was only about thirty miles below the mouth of Clark's Fork.

The trapping parties and free trappers took enormous numbers of beaver and killed many other animals for food or fur. By just the second year of concentrated trapping in the Snake Country, in 1824–1825, the trappers noticed the effects on the streams. On the Bitterroot River in September 1824, Ogden wrote that *"this part of the Country tho' once abounding in Beaver is entirely ruined."* This profoundly disrupted the local ecosystems and native cultures. (Ecological impacts discussed in Chapter 4.)

At times the trappers also stirred up and supported conflict with tribes in the effort to improve their trade. As David Thompson notes in 1811, *"H Cartier the head Chief of the Saleesh Indians, with about twenty men of his tribe also came, these people are the frontier tribe, I strongly requested him to collect his tribe with their allies, the Koo ta naes, Spokane and Skeet shoo Indians who were not far off, he replied, 'you are well aware when we go to hunt the Bison, we also prepare for war with the Pee a gans and their allies; if we had ammunition we should already have been there, for the Cow Bisons are now all fat; but we cannot go with empty Guns; we do not fear War, but we wish to meet our Enemies well armed.'"* He gave all he could spare with a note to Mr. Finan McDonald at the Post to supply them with more ammunition.

The Seliñ attempted to maintain their way of life despite heavy losses from disease and conflict with the Blackfeet and others. Between 1815 and 1820, the Iroquois trappers who came to the territory with the NWC brought word of the powerful "Blackrobes." The Jesuit missionaries had been with the Iroquois in Canada since the 1600s. A Seliñ prophet, Shining Shirt, had experienced a vision of men in long black robes coming to teach them a new way of prayer even before the Iroquois came. In the 1820s and 1830s the Seliñ sent delegations to seek out the Jesuits. They didn't understand that the Jesuits were intent on religious conversion and the elimination of traditional spiritual practices.

The Seliñ were fortunate to have capable leadership. Chief Victor was born in 1790 and became chief in 1841. In the Hells Gate Treaty of 1859 Chief Victor (Many Horses) compelled Isaac Stevens to insert language that defined the Bitterroot Valley south of Lolo Creek as a conditional reservation for the Seliñ. Victor put his mark on the document, convinced that the agreement would not require his people to leave their homeland. Like most treaties signed with first nations this was not to be the case.

Many Horses died on July 4, 1870 while hunting buffalo at the Three Forks of the Missouri River. Charlot, his son, took his place and stood up for their rights. In 1883 Charlot told the government that he would never go to the Jocko reservation alive; that he had no confidence in their promises, *"for,"* said he, *"your Great Father Garfield put my name to a paper which I never signed, and the renegade*

Chief Charlot

Nez Perce, Arlee, is now drawing money to which he has no right. How can I believe you or any white man?"

Charlot and a delegation travelled to Washington, D.C. to present their cases. In response to bribes offered to get him out of the Bitterroot Valley he said that he came to Washington to get the permission of the Great Father to allow him to live unmolested in the Bitterroot Valley, the home of his father and the land of his ancestors. He asked for no assistance from the government except the privilege to remain in the valley where he was born and where the dust of his tribe who lived before him was mingled with the earth. If any of his tribe desired to accept the bounty of the government and remove to the Jocko Reservation he would offer no objection. It was his own wish to live and die in the Bitterroot Valley, where he subsequently died in 1910.

Further challenges came in the way of other broken promises, land grabs, the massacre of the buffalo, commercial salmon harvesting, and dams that blocked the salmon runs. But the Seliñ survived in greater numbers than the coastal tribes, and today 4,000 of their descendants still live on Flathead Indian Reservation in western Montana on the Flathead River, home to the Confederated Salish and Kootenai Tribes of the Flathead Nation. The Salish language is taught at the Nkwusm Salish Immersion School in Arlee, Montana. The southeast Salish peoples of the western United States Plateau region also include Coeur d'Alene, Kalispell, Pend d'Oreille, and Spokane, each with their own subgroups and/or bands all speaking the interior Salish language.

CHUMASH LANDS

CHUMASH

The villages of coastal California astounded early visitors. Almost every village in Chumash territory had its own language and often these were not just different dialects but could be distinctly different languages. The Chumash villages were large, well-organized and full of life, based on intensive resource management. They combined hunting on land and sea with careful plant selection, planting, fishing and gathering. The numerous villages ranged from 50–1500 or more people, and both the coast and islands were well populated. The rich coastal and marine resources, acorns and pine nuts, and many vegetables and grains enabled a complex and very sophisticated society to develop.

The Chumash had highly-developed trade networks, shell bead money, and extensive trail networks. Their capable sea-going canoes facilitated trade and enabled them to fish offshore and

Chumash Village

Interior of Chumash House

Chumash chief

reach the Channel Islands. The prosperous towns enabled them to devote time to cultural development. Sebastian Vizcaino noted in 1602 that the land *"seemed to be all inhabited by Indians."* Somewhere around the Santa Barbara Channel six Chumash came aboard his ship, exchanged gifts, and left.

Juan Rodriguez Cabrillo 1542–43, Pedro de Unamuno in 1587, Sebastián Rodríguez Cermeño in 1595, and Vizcaino in 1602–03 all visited the area. During the 1600s however, the Chumash and their neighbors may also have had contact with Spanish vessels crossing the Pacific and Japanese sailors. Early Spanish maritime voyages may also have interacted with the Chumash and their neighbors and contributed to outbreaks of disease.

Japanese traders and shipwrecks may also have introduced diseases. In 1617, a Japanese junk belonging to Magome was at Acapulco. On October 26, 1613 a Japanese-built trading vessel with Spanish passengers, was sent to Mexico for Masumare, the

Japanese Lord of Oxo, and arrived in Zacatulu, Mexico on January 22, 1614. Mercantile relations between Japan and Mexico continued until 1636. After the restrictions on international shipping, Japanese shipwrecks continued to reach the Pacific Coast, most commonly in Oregon and Washington. However, in 1853, Captain C. M. Scammon discovered the wreck of a Japanese junk on the largest of the San Bonito Island group off Baja California, near Cedros Island. The Alta California newspaper reported several Japanese wrecks adrift or on shore in the 1800s.

Cabrillo's expedition in 1541 spent the most time on the coast. They noted, *"they made use of the Indians, who came on board with water and fish, and appeared very friendly."* Cabrillo wintered over on San Miguel Island during 1542–43 where he died, most likely of gangrene from a wound. Archeological evidence also suggests that Cabrillo introduced a deadly disease to the area.[55] A significant drop in site development and large disorderly burials probably correlate with disease-induced abandonment and consolidation of towns. This could also explain the disappearance of coastal towns named in Cabrillo's log that were gone by the time the missions arrived. Between Point Conception and Las Canoas, the Chumash people provided Cabrillo with names for almost forty mainland towns. The population estimates of 20,000 for pre-contact Chumash neglect the probable impact of early epidemics and I would suggest a better pre-contact estimate may be 30,000 for the Chumash.

In 1587, Pedro de Unamuno had a different reception. A shore party was ambushed by warriors and several men were killed; perhaps they had been remembered as a source of pestilence. Sebastian Rodriquez Cermeño's ill-fated voyage of 1595–1596 provided the coastal people with another exposure to infection. After their ship was wrecked in a storm north of San Francisco Bay, Cermeño and his men coast-hopped south to Mexico in the ship's launch. His entire crew was reported sick at various times, mostly with scurvy but perhaps other diseases as well.

Three ships commanded by Sebastian Vizcaino left Acapulco in May 1602. In November they exchanged goods and food peaceably for ten days with the natives in San Diego. The fleet then sailed northward, but on the ships, *"there were many sick among the men, and some already had died."* Perhaps from scurvy, but again, likely other diseases as well. In December they traded with natives around the Channel Islands and the coast. On December 29, Vizcaino had so many ill men that he sent the sickest back to Mexico on one ship. In January they visited with Chumash again on the way south.

The missions quickly added new diseases,[56] cultural disruption, and loss of resources. They quickly engendered animosity and resistance. Mission San Gabriel Archangel was constructed in 1771, and within a month they had irritated the Chumash's neighbors, the Tongva, enough to be attacked. In 1772, the Franciscans built Mission San Luis Obispo and expanded their reach in the Chumash region. The soldiers accompanying the missions were at times even more of a problem than the priests. In a letter written to the Viceroy of Mexico in 1773, Serra complained that the soldiers would leave in the morning and go to the villages and lasso native women to satisfy their lust. If the native men protested they were shot or beaten.

Thus, continued the destruction of the Chumash. Fur trade vessels made repeated contacts on the California coast from 1790 to 1853. Native hunters from the northern coast working for the Americans and Russians were left on the Channel Islands for several months at a time. With their *baidarkas* they hunted otters around the islands but they could easily reach the coast. These imported hunters probably killed Chumash in conflicts over sea otters, other resources, and women (see the following discussion of the Nicoleño people). Koniag, Unangax, Haida, and Kaigani sea otter hunters, kanakas, as well as Spanish, Russian, American, and British sailors may also have introduced venereal diseases as well as others.

The large villages and dense population centers made the coastal populations very vulnerable to epidemics. Many of these diseases came via ships but they also came overland and spread through the missions. Children were the primary victims of an epidemic of typhoid pneumonia and diphtheria that extended from Monterey to Los Angeles in 1796–1802. In 1806, thousands died of measles, and smallpox swept through in 1829–30.

Even as late as the mission period, there were seven Chumash languages. Harsh living conditions at the missions also led to the spread of disease. In one mission the average life expectancy for a child was just 2.5 years. Two revolts of note took place. In 1785 a Tongva rebellion was attempted by the female shaman, Toypurina; but the conspirators were captured and punished. Unrest continued after Mexican independence when the surviving native people became workers on the newly privatized ranchos. In 1824 the Chumash rose up against the Mexicans after a misunderstanding and fortunately few lives were lost.

When HBC's George Simpson visited California in 1841 he noted, "*In his turn, the Californian treats the savage, wherever he finds him, very much like a beast of prey, shooting him down, even in the absence of any specific charge, as a common pest and a public enemy, and still more decidedly disdaining, in a case of guilt, the aid of such law and justice as the country affords.*"

By 1900 there were only a few hundred dispersed Chumash left. Survivors blended into the community with most working as ranch or farm hands. Only a small reservation was set aside for the Chumash. The Santa Ynez Band of Chumash Mission Indians is the only federally recognized Chumash band. The last fluent native speaker of a Chumash language died in 1965. The Chumash tribe is making progress in recovering their history and taking steps to recover their languages and lost artifacts. In 2010 the Šmuwič Chumash language school was started.

NICOLEÑOS

Evidence shows people had lived on Gha-las-Hat (San Nicolas Island), 70 miles off the coast of southern California, for more than 8,500 years. The islanders faced a challenging environment but

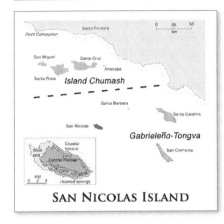

SAN NICOLAS ISLAND

maintained a population of several hundred people. They relied on pelagic fish such as Pacific mackerel, yellowtail, jack mackerel, bill fish, barracuda and ocean sunfish as well as shellfish and marine mammals. With only one small willow tree species on the island they would have been restricted to using balsa boats made with reeds. By 2,000 years ago their hunting efforts had reduced the presence of large sea mammals.

Use of area maps created by archeological studies suggest the people were using all parts of the island intensively. Sites were categorized as follows: 80 residential sites; 79 camp sites; 164 stone artifact manufacture[57] and shellfish processing locations; 90 shellfish processing locations; 100 flaked stone reduction locations; 14 deflated hearth features; and eight sites that were too damaged to be categorized. A high incidence of abnormal bone growth within the ear canal of the remains of San Nicolas islanders suggests they were diving in the cold waters for food.

Food was gathered from the sea

Rainfall was only about nine inches a year, and only a few springs and seeps were found, one accessible only at low tide. Fresh water may have been a concern during droughts.[58] Radiocarbon dates from archeological surveys suggest there was a significant population decrease during the 150-year drought from AD 1100–1250.

The islanders had the short-nosed native dog, and recovered bones show wear patterns suggesting they were important work animals. Careful burials suggest these dogs were also loved and honored companions.

The island was named for Saint Nicholas by Spanish explorer Sebastián Vizcaíno after he sighted the island on December 6, 1602. Other Spanish ships may also have seen and visited the island. During the fur wars traders and hunters visited the island many times in search of sea otters.

The Russians liked the island because it was so far offshore they considered it to be in international waters. They called it Il'mena Island, after the RAC fur trade brig *Il'mena* (and the great lake in Russia). In 1812, Captain Isaac Whittemore of the *Charon* dropped around 50 Koniag (Haida) sea otter hunters on San Nicolas Island for the Russians. They were under the supervision of RAC foreman Iakov Babin.[59] A dispute arose between the Koniags and the residents, originating with the seizure of females by the Koniags. In return, a Koniag hunter was killed, and then the Koniags avenged his death by killing all the native men except for one old man. When a ship returned to pick up the hunters more than a year later (probably the *Il'mena* in the spring of 1814), the island community had been shattered. The men were gone and many of the women had been used by the Koniags as slaves. It is very likely the more attractive women were carried off. Slave trading was not very well regarded, so it was often unreported in journals, ship's logs, and reports.

It took some time for action to be taken. Eventually the Koniags involved in the affair were interviewed by Chief Manager Alexander Baranov. In 1818, his successor L.A. Hagemeister ordered Iakov Babin[60] brought on the *Kutuzov* to Sitka for further questioning. He was then apparently sent on to St. Petersburg. Ivan Kuskov, the manager at Ft. Ross and Babin's boss, was reprimanded for failure to report the massacre to Hagemeister when he was conducting an audit there.

Sea otter and seal hunters from other ships continued to go to the islands. Russian hunters returned to San Nicholas Island in 1815. When Boris Tarasov (RAC) was arrested by the Spanish for hunting sea otter in Spanish waters he said that he had been left in charge of Koniags on the Channel Islands. They had been on San Nicolas for seven months and obtained 955 sea otter skins. Tarasov was eventually freed after traveling to Tepic, Mexico, but the Koniag hunters were kept by the Spanish for two or three years.

A few Nicoleño people survived on the island and a child was born, perhaps the offspring of a native woman and Koniag hunter. More ships came and went as the otters and people became scarcer. In 1835, when the schooner *Peor es Nada* (Nothing is Worse) reached San Nicolas Island to hunt sea otters, they found only 18 surviving natives and took them in to the missions.

Some were enslaved and most, or all, of the others soon died of disease.

In 1843 the brig *Oajaca* headed for the islands with American sea otter hunters Isaac Sparks, George Nidever, and others. The men set to work around San Nicolas and San Clemente Islands, and within a few days they took twenty-one skins. In 1852, Nidever returned to San Nicolas Island and saw footprints. The following year he "rescued" the surviving woman, who was wearing a dress made of green cormorant skins decorated with feathers.[61] She was noted for being friendly, smiling and often singing—quite remarkable after living alone for almost twenty years. Interestingly she could not converse with the Chumash or Tongva people on the coast. She might have

Black balsa were Boats made with reeds waterproofed with asphalt

been a native of the Northwest coast or Alaska, taken to the island to help process skins. She may have been waiting for the return of a fur-trading ship with people she could talk to.

Sadly, she died less than two months later from dysentery. With her may have died the Nicoleño people and their language. We do not know her name or their name for themselves. It is most likely they were Tongva, but that is not certain. The dialects could be so different they seemed like a different language.

RECAP

The impacts of the fur trade on these rich and diverse tribes were catastrophic. The Nicoleño people were gone. Most of the others experienced population declines of up to 90 percent. The treatment by fur traders and governments from all nations was deplorable and often horrific. Yet somehow, most tribes retained a spark of life. They endured further mistreatment after 1840 as settlement occurred, massacres and random killing took place, and treaties were repeatedly broken. Starting in 1860, children were sent away to boarding schools to be remolded as Christian servants and field workers who could not speak their native languages. At the worst point more than 80% of the native children were being taken from their parents. Many of the worst schools were closed in the 1980s and early 1990s.[62]

Today their cultures are being maintained and reinforced through their own initiative. In 1990 Congress passed the Native American Languages Act (NALA) with the goal of recognizing the value of native languages and preventing acts of suppression and extermination directed against Native American languages and cultures.

The federal, provincial, and state governments should be doing much more to recognize the people of the First Nations and to atone for the mistreatment that occurred. The Chinook and Coastal Chumash and Tongva should immediately be recognized as tribes.

WHAT YOU CAN DO!

Get to know your local First Nation. Support their programs to save and reinvigorate the native languages. Support their land claims and lawsuits. Ask for Federal Recognition of tribes that were punished for resisting ill-considered Federal actions. Contribute support for native students schools and colleges including the California Tribal College, Northwest Indian College, Ilisagvik College, Kumeyaay Community College and the Institute of American Indian Arts.

Mission Indian Schools tried to eliminate native languages and beliefs

CHAPTER 4

Ecological Impacts of the Fur Trade

S tudying ecological changes can help us understand the environmental setting we see today and may help us find solutions to some of today's pressing environmental problems. Environmental history is primarily concerned with this relationship between people and the environment. This can be challenging because we have poor records, limited information (archeological sites, pollen, sediments, tree rings, etc.), and a few eyewitness accounts. We are peering into a dim and darkened room.

These management problems are not new, and we can learn from the First Nations successes and failures. The people of the Fur Coast were intelligent, skilled and knowledgeable applied ecologists who managed their environments well for thousands of years. They made mistakes as well, and sometimes extracted more from the environment than it could maintain. However, the fur trade impacts were at an entirely different scale and were as catastrophic to the ecosystems of the area as the diseases were for the people. Sea otters and beaver are key species and ecosystem managers. Their removal triggered trophic cascades of decline that we still see today.

A better knowledge of the fur trade can help improve our use and management of the land and sea. It will also support commercial resource extraction while protecting rare and endangered ecosystems and species.

To manage lands effectively we need to appreciate what impacts our ancestors had, how they interacted with global changes in climate, and how they failed or succeeded in their efforts. A better understanding may also help us survive on our small Spaceship Earth.

The discussion begins with the sea otter, then the beaver, and finally other species.

SEA OTTERS

Sea otters *(Enhydra lutris)* have little or no body fat. To survive they maintain an exceptionally high metabolic rate and rely on their dense fur for insulation. This valuable fur was their undoing. The fur consists of an outer layer of protective guard hairs with extremely fine dense under fur of approximately a million hairs per square inch. Oil from glands in the skin helps to enhance the water repellency of the fur but sea otters must groom their fur frequently to maintain the air barrier and its insulative quality.

Males and females are usually segregated. Adult females usually haul out in favored sheltered places near the extremities of points. Males, except those actively seeking to mate, may limit feeding activities to a radius of several hundred meters from their preferred haul-out location if plenty of food is availability. Mating may occur year-round, but in Prince William Sound it peaked in fall. Females typically first breed at four years of age and can pup annually. They generally separate from their pup before mating. Birth usually takes place in the water and typically produces a single pup. Twins do occur but both rarely survive.

Males establish and maintain breeding territories to prolong precopulatory interactions that encourage female–pup separation. Their post-copulatory interactions help prevent females from mating with another male. Male mating success was found to be related to age, weight, territory quality, and the length of time they maintained their territory.

Although each adult and independent juvenile forages alone, sea otters tend to rest together in single-sex groups called rafts. A raft typically contains 10 to 100 animals, with male rafts being larger than female ones. Rafts of up to 400 otters have been seen

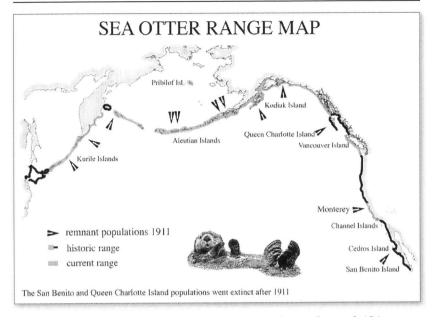

SEA OTTER RANGE MAP

Pribilof Isl.

Kodiak Island

Aleutian Islands

Queen Charlotte Island

Vancouver Island

Kurile Islands

Monterey

Channel Islands

Cedros Island

San Benito Island

➤ remnant populations 1911
historic range
current range

The San Benito and Queen Charlotte Island populations went extinct after 1911

and were perhaps once very common. To keep from drifting out to sea when resting and eating, sea otters may wrap themselves in kelp. Rafting promotes social interaction and likely enhances food finding and provides some protection from predators. But rafting can also increase the spread of disease.

During grooming, the fur is cleaned, hair shafts are straightened and aligned to maintain loft, oil is distributed and air is blown through the fur where it is trapped as tiny bubbles for insulation. Vigorous grooming generally occurs before and after feeding and rest periods. Maintaining the fur water/air barrier is critical for young pups who need special care to stay warm. Mothers may lick and fluff a newborn for hours until the pup floats like a cork before she goes hunting. The fluffy baby fur is replaced by adult fur after about three months.

Sea otters once ranged from Northern Japan across the North Pacific to central Baja California (Map 1). Archeological research has shown that the otters were widely used by native communities for both fur and food. But the harvest was below the level that would harm this species. This all changed with the arrival of the commercial sea otter hunters, and within a few years they were wiped out on the Aleutian Islands. Ultimately they were hunted almost to extinction during the fur rush. The total removal of sea otters was at least 500,000 and perhaps as much as a million. At the low point the estimate is that less than 2,000 (much less than 1% of the pre-fur trade population) survived in thirteen remnant populations in 1911. Several of these remnant populations, including those in the Queen Charlotte Islands, declined to extinction after 1911. The last verified sea otter in Canada was shot near Kyuquot, British Columbia in 1929. They have since returned.

It is uncertain what the otter populations and kelp beds were like in California before sea otter hunting began. A 1976 California Department of Fish and Game report estimated the historic population might had been 16,000. A finer-grained but equally flawed study in 1996 suggested even less. Neither carefully considered the 50,000 otters taken in California by hunters or the catastrophic decline in kelp beds, invertebrates, fish populations, and habitat quality along the coast with the fur trade. A historical study of the Palos Verde kelp forest showed a maximum extent in 1928 of almost 2,500 acres; this dropped to a low of four acres in 1974. It is fairly clear that California kelp may occupy only about a tenth of the range measured in 1911—a huge loss for sea otters.

I would suggest there were probably 30,000 sea otters in California pre-contact. Within 50 years of the start of hunting, the populations had crashed. In California they were thought to be extinct until a small group of 50 was rediscovered on the central coast. This is a survival rate of only 0.2%. In recent years California has about 3,000 sea otters.

Small remnant populations also survived on a few of the Aleutian and Kurile Islands and the coast of Kamchatka. After intense hunting stopped they became re-established in some areas. They managed to return to some of the Aleutian Islands and by the 1980s, the population in Alaska was estimated at 50,000. Sadly, the population collapsed again in the late 1980s and 1990s. For example, the Rat Islands Group were one of the areas with a surviving remnant population in 1911. Rat Island itself had 270 otters in 1959, 326 in 1965, and 79 in 1992, but only 11 in 2000. This compares with 955 taken by Russian hunters over seven months during the soft gold rush.

By 2003 some estimates suggested the total Alaska sea otter population had declined to less than 9,000. From near carrying capacity in some areas in 1965 the population had fallen 50–99% in different parts of the Aleutian Islands. After 2003 the population appears to have stabilized but not grown. The reasons for this general decline are not well understood. The population decline occurred across the archipelago, suggesting a common and geographically widespread cause. It may reflect the complex effects of climate change or the impacts of overfishing. It has even been suggested that killer whales are eating more sea otters as other prey have declined. Large areas to the south of the Gulf of Alaska, with the exception of California, remain unoccupied.

KEYSTONE SPECIES EFFECTS

The sea otter is a keystone species, playing a critical role in the near shore ecosystems from Baja California to the Aleutians. They prefer rocky bottoms and reefs but are found in areas of Prince William Sound and southwestern Bristol Bay where the bottom is composed exclusively of soft sediments. Sea otters forage primarily on invertebrates, which they obtain by diving to the sea floor. They hold rocks to their chest and can break even sturdy clams. They can be seen out as far as 100-foot depths but prefer shallower water.

California sea otters preferentially associate with giant kelp as opposed to bull kelp. Specific kelp beds are used as habitual rafting sites for groups of otters as well as for individuals. Kelp beds are also used for foraging and are important, but not required, habitat components. They were probably once more common on soft sediments in the southern oceans as well, but with the overhunting of bivalves, abalone, and fish they could no longer survive in these areas.

Sea otters regulate the abundance and size of their prey. By preying on herbivores such as sea urchins, sea otters reduce grazing pressure and increase algal abundance. Sea otters can help restore kelp beds (and associated ecosystems). Sea otters in California have been seen to completely remove large sea urchins from areas by predation, permitting luxuriant development of the kelp forests. Scientists studying sea otters found that Amchitka Island had very dense kelp beds. The kelp was so abundant that they could not see the rocky ocean floor either from the shore or when diving in the water. On islands without sea otters there was little kelp but immense numbers of sea urchins.

The removal of the sea otter was to have dire consequences for the kelps. Predation on kelps increased and kelp forests declined. In recently re-occupied rocky habitats where sea urchins are abundant, sea urchins are consumed preferentially by sea otters, probably because of ease of capture. Studies of otters near Pacific Grove, California showed they were each eating more than 100 urchins a day. They were found to preferentially eat more nutritious urchins rather than those from urchin barrens.

As the abundance of preferred species declines, the sea otter diet diversifies to include a larger array of invertebrates, including various bivalves, snails, chitons, crabs, sea stars, and fish in some areas. Clams are an important part of the sea otter diet in Southeast Alaska and British Columbia. In other areas squid may be important, and sea otters have been seen taking surf scoters (small birds).

The kelp beds and kelp forests enhance nearshore productivity and when kelp dies it enters the food webs as detritus from drift algae and dissolved organic material. This can be critically important for abalone and other snails and shellfish.

At islands in the Aleutian chain that were dominated by sea otters, kelp-derived carbon accounted for more than half the carbon in food webs. Nearshore productivity was two to five times higher in areas with sea otters and kelp.

Re-introducing sea otters is a challenge because the kelp forest is so important for the sea otters. If there is little or no kelp it can be hard for them to survive long enough to clear out the urchin hordes. It may also take time for the kelp to return. The recovery in Monterey Bay was remarkable and took less than 10 years.

Once the kelp is established there is more food available for the otters. The kelps also provide protection for the otters and they often wrap themselves in kelp while resting or sleeping. A mother may wrap her pup in kelp so she can go hunting. A restoration effort should start with a kelp planting effort or installation of artificial kelps.

The recent decline of many species, including sea otters, in the North Pacific may be a result of climate change. Extreme oceanic regime shifts include increased variability in sea surface temperatures and changes in salinity. Population declines of sea otters, Steller sea lions, whiskered auklets, Pacific Ocean perch, red king crabs and other species are not well understood. However, less food for sea otters can be critical for a species that needs 190 calories per kg per day (that would be 19,000 calories a day for me). This can represent eating 20–30% of their body weight per day and if food sources or food quality declines, the effect can be deadly. Sea otters must maintain a high metabolism to stay warm and can easily die of exposure. Late winter deaths from starvation have been observed in many areas.

Sea otters also face some risks from Paralytic Shellfish Poisoning caused by dinoflagellate species. This poison can accumulate to toxic levels in filter-feeding bivalves and has led to large die-offs in the Kodiak Archipelago. Domoic acid can also accumulate in shellfish. This is caused by a single-celled toxic algae *(Pseudo-nitzschia)*. Sea otters are able to reduce risk of poisoning from domoic acid by selecting less toxic shellfish, perhaps by smell. Domoic acid can cause seizures, memory loss, even death in people and other mammals. It has been identified as the cause of several large die-offs of sea birds and sea lions and suspected in the death of sea otters.

Many California sea otters have also been killed by toxoplasmosis (*T. gondii*) from cat feces. The unexpected connection between cats and the ocean environment was found to be a major cause of mortality of sea otters in some areas. A seroprevalence analysis showed that 52% of 305 freshly dead sea otters found on beaches were infected.

Increased predation also appears to be a growing risk. Killer whales and sleeper and salmon sharks are suspected to be eating more sea otters than they did historically. Decreases in other foods and fish from over-fishing and climate change may have led to broader selection of prey—including sea otters. Bald eagles can prey on otter pups.

Other risks include poachers, oil spills (3–4,000 died in the Exxon Valdez oil spill), industrial pollution, agricultural chemicals, fishing gear, collisions, noise pollution, and inadequate food from commercial and sport fishing, invertebrate harvesting, and climate change. The increased temperatures of the sea surface in the North Pacific (up to 7°F in recent studies) can reduce upwelling of nutrient rich sea water and collapse the food chain.

Sea otters may also be shot or speared by fishermen or vandals. Captain Howard Shelby of the California Department of Fish and Game reported that in one period (late 1957 to early 1958) in the Monterey area alone eighteen dead otters were found. "Some had a hole clear through them, either spear or bullet wound."

SEA OTTER REINTRODUCTION

Restoration efforts have been made in many areas with modest success. Sea otters are unlikely to survive without kelp forests so one of the first steps is restoring kelps. Experience shows this can be done but is not easy. The most persistent kelp beds appear to occur on solid rock substrate with moderately low relief and moderate coverage by sand. In one restoration effort the highest density of kelp was on larger boulders that provided sufficient stability for growth and development of the young sporophytes.

Sea otters have been intentionally reintroduced in several areas. Re-introductions to southeast Alaska, British Columbia, Washington and Oregon were attempted in the 1960s and 1970s. Sea otters have slowly spread along Vancouver Island and some coastal areas of British Columbia, survived in northern Washington, but failed to take in Oregon. The Alaska efforts were generally successful.

An attempt to return them to San Nicolas Island led to a long swim, as 36 returned 180 miles to the central coast of California where they had been captured. Others fell prey to sharks and orcas. A small resident population of about 80 have survived. No efforts to return others to the Baja California coast have been made but individuals have been seen along the coast.

Between 1967 and 1980, kelp restoration was conducted along the Palos Verdes Peninsula by the Institute of Marine Resources and the California Department of Fish and Game. This work combined sea urchin control and kelp transplanting, with the hope of establishing several small stands of giant kelp that would provide seed stock for new and expanding beds. In 1974, the first naturally expanding kelp stand in 20 years was observed off the Palos Verdes Peninsula. By 1980, when restoration work was discontinued, the stand covered nearly 600 acres. Today the forests typically range from 500–700 acres.

In another project, more than 3 million urchins were removed over four years, reducing the density from 18.5 purple urchins per square meter to 1.4. It helped, but the cost of continuous urchin removal and kelp planting would be very high for the entire coast. Ocean Cove was the location of the Watermen's Association first urchin removal event on Memorial Day weekend in 2018. One hundred divers removed 56,000 purple sea urchins from the cove in an attempt to help the kelps return.

In the worst areas, with 100 sea urchins per square meter, the cost of removal would be staggering. Off the northern California coast an urchin removal vacuum cleaner has been developed. Diver Jon Holcomb found he could clear almost a tennis court-sized area in two hours. Faster than hand cleaning, but he admits, "It's much like trying to scratch the paint off a house with a pin," says Holcomb. "It's not gonna be easy."

Marine biologist Nancy Caruso has addressed the cost issue by working with local high school students to raise juvenile giant kelp in their classrooms and then out-planting the kelp with volunteer divers. One project included 5,000 students (ages 11 to 18) and 250 skilled volunteer divers. They planted kelp in fifteen different areas off the coast of Orange County. Only one spot near Dana Point had kelp that could serve as a resource base. They collected reproductive blades from these kelp and the students cleaned them. Then they were left out of water in the refrigerator overnight, covered with paper towels. The next morning they were put in ice-cold seawater and the "shocked" kelp blade would release millions of spores. (These are 400 times smaller than you can see.) The spores would land on small ceramic bathroom tiles where students would raise the kelp in the classroom nurseries for about four months. At this point you can see them with your naked eye, and then they are then set out in the ocean by divers.

In Tasmania, lobsters were reintroduced to help control urchins. On isolated patches of urchin barrens this really helped. Lobsters may eat about 900 urchins per acre every month. On big kelp barrens, you could deposit large lobsters that will eat thousands of urchins but they may not be able to reduce the population enough for any kelp to reappear.

Recent commercial edible kelp farming projects offer new hope for rapid establishment of kelp using submerged cables and strings with young kelp established in a lab. These may enable kelp to be returned to areas at low cost, but challenges still remain. The decline of kelp forests exhibits many of the problems facing restoration ecologists. You can't easily fix the kelp ecosystem by just considering kelp and otters. A good kelp forest needs sheephead fish, sea stars, crabs, clams, lobsters and more. Trying to return just one element can help but is likely to require persistent and costly efforts on several fronts for success. A combined sea urchin removal effort and seeding with kelp culture may help start recovery, but the goal should be to restore the sea otter population, allow sheephead and lobster numbers to increase, and to reduce the discharge of stormwater, pollutants, nutrients, and hot water into coastal waters.

Once the urchins are diminished and the kelp is healthy, otters can be re-introduced to continue suppression of purple urchins and other kelp eaters. Marine sanctuary status can help by increasing predation on urchins by lobsters, crabs and fish.

A comprehensive plan for kelp restoration along the Pacific Coast is long overdue. Improved understanding of the methods for growing kelp also make it more likely that successful reintroductions can be made. An ocean-based section of the California Conservation Corps could provide training and jobs for hundreds of young men and women removing urchins and growing and transplanting kelp.

BEAVERS

Beavers are highly social, adaptable and energetic mammals, probably second only to humans in their effect on the environment. The North American beaver *(Castor canadensis)* was once very common and widely distributed, with populations estimated as high as 400 million in North America before European settlement, trapping, hunting and habitat loss. They ranged from habitat as hot as the Colorado River in the deserts of Arizona and California and the Gulf of Mexico and Florida to the far north of Alaska and Canada. In a few areas beaver were considered related to humans and treated kindly.

Recent research in California has revealed a much broader historic range for beaver than previous studies suggested. They had been so thoroughly trapped out it was thought they had never been there at all. In 1829, Hudson's Bay Company trappers from Oregon took 4,000 beaver skins from the shores of San Francisco Bay. By using fur trade notes, pioneer accounts, newspaper articles, and archeological and physical evidence, the former range of beaver was extended to almost all of California except the driest desert (Map 2).

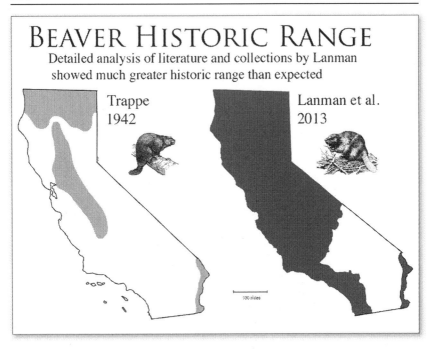

BEAVER HISTORIC RANGE
Detailed analysis of literature and collections by Lanman
showed much greater historic range than expected

Trappe
1942

Lanman et al.
2013

100 miles

Beaver are large rodents with very sharp, tough front teeth that grow continuously and sharpen against each other. These ivory chisels are used to cut trees and collect bark for food. Beaver can reach 4–6 feet in length and weigh as much as 50–90 pounds or more. Strong muscles are helpful for moving wood. The front legs are rather short but able to grasp and manipulate items, while the rear legs are larger and stronger with webs to aid in swimming. The two inside rear toes are specially designed for grooming. Beaver produce the yellowish secretion, castoreum, in two sacks between the pelvis and the tailbone. The paddle-like tail is flattened and scaly and up to ten inches long. Not only used as a rudder, the tail can produce a warning slap when danger is perceived. Beaver can dive for up to fifteen minutes at a time.

Beaver waddle along, standing upright unless frightened, when they can move faster in a rather awkward gallop. Their slow speed makes them vulnerable on land and they try to develop and use ponds, slides, and canal systems to stay in the water as much as possible. Beaver are most active at dawn and dusk but will also work at

Beaver dams can be quite large.

night. Some early reports suggest they were more active in the day-time before hunting and trapping nearly exterminated them.

Beaver will typically live 10–15 years but can reach 30 years of age. They form long-term pair bonds and usually breed in winter, giving birth to 2–4 kits in the spring. Under good conditions a female may give birth at age two or three; older mothers tend to have larger, more successful litters. The kits are able to swim after just four days, eat predominately solid food at the age of one month, and are able to dive by eight weeks. They may stay with the parents for up to two years or longer to learn how to be a successful beaver. Dispersing beaver face many risks in relocation, particularly if their journey is partly over land.

Beavers are social and will live in colonies if given the chance. This may be simply a large family group of adults, subadults and kits, or a group of related beaver on adjacent territories; this can include several generations as well. Grooming is a favorite social activity, done mainly inside the house for safety.

Some very large dams have enabled several families to live in the same pond. I have seen a number of houses in use even on a relatively small lake. Dominance has been suggested to be matriarchal or size-related. Scent marking is used to define territories and little mounds may be set up as markers.

Beaver are highly adaptable and can survive and prosper in very difficult environments ranging from the Colorado River in the desert to the Yukon in northern Alaska. I have seen a beaver living at a lake at 10,000 feet in the Rockies with nothing but small willows and herbs to eat. I have also seen an urban beaver living in a polluted and grocery cart-filled creek in Portland. However, the most enterprising beaver I have seen was developing a dam and canal system on a small creek on a side slope near Lizard Head Peak high in the Colorado Rockies.

A beaver family will set up their home on a lake or small-to-medium sized creek with relatively low gradients. If sufficient material is available the house is elegantly designed and stoutly built of sticks and mud with the living quarters accessible only by submerged entrances. This will be set out in the lake or pond if possible, but when the lake is too deep, the river is too swift, or if materials are short, it may be set on the bank or simply tunneled into the bank. The Colorado River beaver homes are typically bank tunnels.

Dam building provides the basis for the saying "busy as a beaver." Beaver will build quite elaborate dams and canal systems to manage water and improve their quality of life. Downstream branches are set sharp end down and then a complex web of sticks are strategically placed, with vegetation and mud used to hold the water back. Even with small streams, the density of beaver

Beaver at work

dams can be remarkable. I have seen a stretch of creek in Colorado with 30+ dams in a very small area. Tests suggest that beaver are effectively programmed to build when they hear the sound of rushing water; special silent water bypasses can help keep beaver from flooding roads and neighborhoods. Beaver also devote many hours of work in the late summer to caching food for winter, which they store underwater near the lodge. Aspen and maple were preferred foods in Ontario caches. It can be deadly if they run out, as gathering food on foot over the snow makes them very much at risk.

Beaver will primarily eat bark if they can get it, with aspen, poplar, and cottonwood favored. They also enjoy leaves and bulbs from some species, with water lilies being a particular favorite. In other locations beaver have relied on poisonous plants. The Malad River in Oregon got its name from beaver meat that made trappers sick. Beaver digestion is improved by a special cardio-gastric gland and a large cecum with microbial populations to help digest the woody materials. When possible they store a large collection of preferred trees and food at the bottom of their beaver pond for use over winter.

Beaver may be a preferred food for wolves in some areas. Mountain lions, coyotes, bears, wolverines, jaguars, lynx, bobcat, and even river otters may also prey on beaver. The lodges offer good protection, particularly when they are frozen in winter. However, if beaver are forced to bring in food overland in winter they are very vulnerable.

Humans have been the predominant predator. Beaver were hunted by natives for food and fur for thousands of years before Europeans arrived. When felt hats became popular around 1800, the rush was on because the interlocking hairs made beaver fur an ideal source for felt hats. The best fur quality was found from late fall to spring. Beaver trapping in the Northwest was pursued vigorously to exterminate the beaver and create a fur desert to slow American's westward push. As Governor George Simpson wrote to John McLoughlin in July 1826, *"It is intended that a strong Trapping Expedition be kept up to hunt in the country to the southward of the*

Columbia ... and to leave it in as bad a state as possible." The impact of heavy trapping was described by Peter Skene Ogden in the Snake River country on May 28, 1829. "*It is scarcely credible what a destruction of beaver by trapping this season, within the last few days upwards of fifty females have been taken and on an average each with four young ready to litter.*" They quickly drew down and often wiped out the beaver populations taking males, females, and young. Peter Skene Ogden felt some remorse. "*It is almost a sin to see the number of small beaver we destroy and to no purpose. Some of the females taken have no less than five young... [and] rivers subject to overflow their banks require double and treble the time to recruit after being trapped.*" As John McLoughlin noted in 1837, "*The (Sacramento) valley, itself, with the numerous streams owing into it, from the surrounding mountains have all been visited and their stores of Beaver considerably reduced.*" David Thompson noted that on the Canoe River a trapper had taken 850 beaver in one winter, but that after a second season they would be gone.

Beaver activity is easily identified and trappers became very skilled in catching them. Female beavers do not mature for three years and do not produce successful, large litters until even later, so a repeated trapping effort can easily wipe out a population. As the adults were trapped out, any young beaver left behind would often be unable to fend for themselves. Widely dispersed survivors would have trouble finding each other and even if a colony restarted it would often be taken in the next year or two as the trappers returned. The rapid decline in population can be seen in decreasing returns from the Snake River country and the California parties. In one case when they revisited a previously trapped area they got only two beaver instead of eighty.

The total number of beaver taken in Alaska, the West, and Northwest will never be known accurately as many were illegally trapped or traded, and reports are often fragmented and unclear about the origin and destination of the furs. Records in California are limited because virtually all of the parties were in the field illegally or attempting to avoid taxes and tariffs. Many beaver were killed but not recovered when the traps were not set correctly. Beaver skins were also lost or damaged in transit and not recorded. We do know that The Russian American Company collected more than 200,000 beaver pelts from Alaska and the Northwest Coast from 1798–1842. The Hudson's Bay Company took more than more than 400,000 beaver from the Northwest. The beaver take on the Missouri was about 375,000 just from 1815–1830, with many of these from the mountains and some from the Northwest. And finally, perhaps 50,000 beaver were trapped in California, and many others in Arizona, New Mexico and Utah. By the 1840s beaver populations were considerably reduced throughout the West and many populations had been wiped off the face of the earth.

Trapping continued into the 20th century when only an estimated 1,000 beaver remained in California. They were protected in 1911 but faced continued hunting, trapping, and loss of habitat. It had indeed become a fur desert.

Castoreum was also harvested and used as bait for trapping. It was used until recent times as a scent enhancer in perfumes and as a food additive because it offered the scent of vanilla or strawberries. For more than eighty years castoreum could be found in some ice cream, gums, and other foods as a "natural flavor." Traditionally it was considered a useful medicine. These days, castoreum is primarily used for fragrances because it is too expensive to use in food.

KEYSTONE SPECIES EFFECTS

The removal of beaver initiated change in watersheds and ecosystems through the beaver lands, reaching from the San Francisco Bay area, south to the southern San Joaquin Valley, along the western Sierra streams, through the coast range north to Oregon and throughout northern California. Beaver were wiped out on the east side of the Sierra. The Sacramento River delta and San Francisco Bay were particularly rich in beaver as Thomas Farnham noted, *"There is probably no spot of equal extent on the whole continent of America, which contains so many of these much sought after animals."*

Beaver play important hydrologic and ecological roles in watersheds, and their removal leads to undesirable changes. A research project in Wyoming released ten beaver into a river where they had been absent and by the following year they had constructed 55 dams. Not all beaver had dams or lived where dams were possible but removing as many as 750,000 beaver from the West may have taken out more than 2 million dams. In California, taking 50,000 beaver may have led to the loss of more than 100,000 dams.

These beaver dams are ecologically very important. They slow water loss from ecosystems, reduce stream velocity, and minimize erosive power during flood peak flows. Beaver dams also raise and stabilize the surrounding water table, which creates ideal conditions for riparian plants and trees. The often-extensive beaver canals and channels also help spread water across flood plains and increase the area of wetland and riparian plant species.

All of these factors are critical in the drylands of the west. By helping to maintain wetlands they improve water quality and enhance fish habitat in streams by increasing water depth, maintaining refuges of deeper, cooler water, and improving stream flow. They also provide improved habitat for waterfowl, big game, and game birds, and improve habitat for other wildlife through vegetative growth. Duck populations, for example, were seventy-five times higher on streams with beaver dams in a paired study comparison in Wyoming.

Dams in the arid west are more short-lived than those in the north, often lasting only a few years before they are abandoned or washed out and need to be rebuilt or moved. Water storage starts to decline quickly after the beaver are gone; within a week or two the water level will drop six inches to a foot as maintenance work stops. In low gradient streams or rivers this can lead to a rapid loss of wetlands. When a flood causes a dam failure, erosion can be locally severe as a large pond drains rapidly, adding to the flood flow.

Even if the beaver ponds are maintained they may fill in, creating first a shallow marsh and then grassy meadows that may provide unique and rather rare habitats in arid and semi-arid areas. Studies in Montana showed that a beaver dam may be filled in completely within ten to fifteen years. Summer stream flows often decline or cease after the dams are abandoned.

The dam-building and foraging of the beaver also shape ecosystems in other ways. If beaver population densities are high, then cottonwoods, aspen, and other favored food species may be over-harvested, causing long-term habitat to decline for beavers. This can be seen as a field of stumps with a tree line of palatable trees so far from the pond that the beavers will no longer cross it. The beavers may have to move on to a new location.

The ecological dance between wolves, elk, and beaver illustrates the complexity of interaction between species that might not be considered related. Studies in the Yellowstone ecosystem have shown a dramatic link between wolves and beaver. When the grey wolf was

Water conservation in beaver ponds

reintroduced into the Greater Yellowstone ecosystem in 1995, there were 44 beaver colonies in the northern range of the park; in 2007 there were 127 with the promise of more to come. When wolves were re-introduced they changed elk behavior and population density. Keeping the elk out of the riparian areas allowed willows and cottonwoods to thrive, allowing beaver to return. The dams, in turn, create riparian areas that offered more food for elk.

BEAVER RESTORATION

Although the value of returning beavers to their former range is not a new idea, it has gained importance in the last ten years. After decades of neglect and ignorance beavers are being appreciated for their many ecological benefits. Reintroductions are being made and impacts are being studied more carefully. Strategies for living with beavers are also being developed to avoid unwanted flooding and blocking of drain pipes.

One of the early restoration efforts involved parachuting beavers in to the Idaho wilderness in the 1940s. Today more reintroductions are being made and the benefits are being studied more carefully. Problem beavers are more likely to be relocated instead of killed.

Returning beaver to watersheds has brought water to streams that once dried up in summer. Reduced flood intensity has led to channel filling, reduced erosion, and stabilized river banks. The changes in river flow and channel stability and increased areas of open water and wetlands have benefitted a wide range of plant, insect, animal and bird species.

Nutrient capture and retention by beaver ponds is also important and can improve stream water quality and ecosystem health. Total nitrogen increased 72% in a watershed with beaver, while the more available form of nitrate nitrogen more than doubled. Organic matter increased threefold after beaver dams were built. Phosphorus loss from the ecosystem was cut by two-thirds. These combined effects typically improve productivity and reduce water pollution.

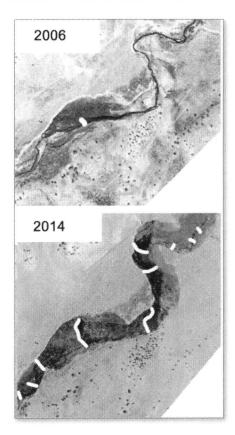

Beaver dams on Susie Creek Nevada conserve water and increase vegetation.

Beaver reintroduction is not always easy or even possible without human help. Artificial check dams may be needed to hold water long enough for plants and trees to grow large enough to support beavers. Become a beaver supporter and foster watershed recovery. Encouraging beaver to build dams and create ponds is an affordable and effective habitat restoration technique. It is possible to use passive actions such as trapping restrictions or changes in grazing management to increase food for beavers; simple relocation to help establish colonies; relocating beaver after installing stream-stabilizing check dams and planting preferred food species. They usually will do better if an established family is moved together rather than relocating unrelated individuals.

OTHER FUR SPECIES

The sea otter and beaver provided the most important skins on the Pacific Coast but they were not the only animals hunted. The first animal hunted to extinction was the sea cow—in just 27 years. As the sea otter populations declined, hunting for fur seals became more important. They were low in value but enormous numbers were killed. Sea lions were hunted so hard in the north that skins had to be brought up from California for *baidarka* covers. Land animals other than beaver were also taken in large numbers and ecological cascades of change resulted in many areas. Sadly, the effects of these changes have been little studied. Here is a short summary of the loss.

STELLER'S SEA COW

Steller's sea cows *(Hydrodamalis gigas)* were very large relatives of the manatee that could reach 30 feet in length and weigh 4–10 tons. The large size and blubber layers reduced heat loss and energy demand in these cold climates.

Steller's sea cow had a relatively small head, a broad horizontal forked tail fluke, and small, stumpy hook-shaped front flippers. Steller said these were used to pull the sea cow along in shallow water as it collected and ate algae. The bark-like skin was dark brown, sometimes streaked or spotted with white. The nostrils were near the tip of the snout, the eyes were relatively small, and many large bristles surrounded the mouth. Sea cows used horny plates in the mouth to compact kelp and other big algae collected at or near the ocean's surface along shore. Steller felt that they were monogamous and described a male staying near its wounded mate and trying to free her. Offspring were observed to be born at any time

Steller's sea cow

of year. The sea cows had little ability to submerge and were easy targets for hunters.

In the distant past Steller's sea cow ranged from the northern Japanese archipelago to the Pacific coast of Baja California—about the same as sea otters when Europeans arrived. But sea cows had disappeared across most of this range long before the first Russian hunters arrived, probably from hunting by native people. The largest population was in the Commander Islands but it is possible some also persisted in the western Aleutian Islands into the 18th century. Aleut oral history suggests that sea cows had historically inhabited the most remote western Aleutian Islands. Evidence of a population on St. Lawrence Island in the northern Bering Sea from more than a thousand years ago has also been found. They had probably survived on the Commander Islands because the islands were not permanently occupied. No one knows how many sea cows still survived in the Commander Islands when Steller arrived, but it may have been only 1,500 or less.

Fortunately for Georg Wilhelm Steller, sea cows were still living on Bering Island when they ship wrecked on the island in 1741. They proved essential food for the crew. Steller describes how they were hunted and says the meat was similar to beef in taste and texture. He said the blubber surpassed the best beef fat and was the color of olive oil. Another source suggested that one sea cow could feed thirty men for a month. The blubber was used for oil lamps and the thick, tough hide was used for shoes, belts and skin-covered boats.

The *Trinity* arrived in 1762 on Bering's Island and stayed until the first of August 1763. They killed about 500 arctic foxes, just 20 sea otters and several sea cows for the coverings of their *baydars*.[63]

In the mid-1700s some of the Russian *promyshlenniki* would winter on Bering Island and they killed sea cows to eat over the winter and to put up as food for the next summer hunt. Their methods were crude and injured animals were often lost. Petr Yakolev, who wintered over in 1754, noted that the sea cows were already gone from Copper Island. On previous trips they had seen hundreds of sea otters and many sea cows, but now the cows were gone. Yakolev also noted that the men said the sea cabbage (algae) the sea cows fed on was gone as well. Yakolev recommended that the Bolsheretsk Chancellery immediately forbid further hunting of sea cows so that, *"they will not be exterminated from Commander (Bering) Island."* Sadly, his report did not stop the slaughter.

The extinction may have been accelerated by the virtual elimination of sea otters and resulting increases in sea urchins and loss of kelp. Kelp and other big fleshy algae were the sea cow's primary food source in the North Pacific while seagrasses might have provided food in other areas. The first bones of a Steller's sea cow were unearthed about 70 years after it was presumed extinct. Since then many hundreds of bones have been found and skeletons have been assembled for museums. Bones continue to be unearthed in the Commander Islands.

FUR SEALS (SEVERAL SPECIES)

In the North Pacific, most sealing took place after the sea otters were severely depleted. Fur seals are very vulnerable on land, where they breed and have their young and can easily be bludgeoned to death. Hundreds of thousands of fur seals lined coasts and offshore islands in cold water areas throughout the world. The Northern Fur Seal (*Callorhinus ursinus*) population was estimated at 4.5 million in 1870, but sealing had reduced them to 200,000 by 1914. The 2000 IUCN Red List of Threatened Species lists it as Vulnerable, the category below Endangered, after a sharp and alarming decline. The species spends much of the year in open sea, and there has been speculation that in addition to reduced food from overfishing, losses from entanglements in fishing nets and gear, and illegal killing by fishing and other vessels may be to blame.

The Guadalupe Fur Seal (*Arctocephalus townsendi*) was hunted almost to extinction before researchers knew they existed. Guadalupe fur seals were not identified as a distinct species until 1897. They were found on the islands off the Baja coast, the Channel

Islands, and the Farallons. The original population has been estimated as high as 200,000. They are similar to northern fur seals in appearance but are slightly smaller, and the males are lighter brown. Guadalupe fur seals are pelagic, living almost all of the time in the open ocean.

Guadalupe fur seals were thought to be extinct until 1926, when a few dozen were discovered on Guadalupe Island. Several seals were sent to the San Diego Zoo in 1928, but after a quarrel between one of the fishermen and the zoo director, the fisherman stormed off to Guadalupe Island to kill the entire herd. He killed every seal he found and sold the skins in Panama, where he was killed in a barroom fight. Fortunately, he didn't kill them all, and in 1954, a small colony of 14 was found. In 1975 Guadalupe Island was declared a sanctuary for pinnipeds by the Mexican government because of the presence of the fur seals and two other pinnipeds, the Northern Elephant Seal *(Mirounga angustirostris)* and the California sea lion *(Zalophus californianus)*. In 2010 the population was estimated at about 20,000 in Mexico, but it is still considered an endangered species. Fur seals are killed by gill nets and other fishing tackle, and are also shot by fishermen.

SEA LIONS

The Steller sea lion (*Eumetopias jubatus*) was first described by Georg Wilhelm Steller in 1741. The former range of the Steller sea lion is like that of sea otters, extending from the Kuril Islands and the

Sea of Okhotsk in Russia to the Gulf of Alaska in the north, and south to the Channel Islands and perhaps to Mexico. Steller sea lions forage near shore and in pelagic waters and can travel long distances with the ability to dive to approximately 1300 feet. They use land habitat as

Steller's sea lion

haul-out sites for periods of rest, molting, and as rookeries for mating and pupping during the breeding season. At sea, they are seen
alone or in small groups but may gather in large "rafts" at the surface near rookeries and haul-outs. Steller sea lions are opportunis-
tic predators, foraging and feeding primarily at night on a wide variety of fishes (e.g., capelin, cod, herring, mackerel, pollock, rockfish,
salmon, sand lance, etc.), bivalves, cephalopods (e.g., squid and
octopus) and gastropods.

Sea lions were heavily hunted for their meat, fur, skins, oil, and
various other products. In the 19th century their whiskers sold for
a penny apiece for use as tobacco-pipe cleaners. Later they were
killed and bountied because fishermen blamed them for stealing
fish (in the early 1900s). In more recent years they have been illegally killed to limit their predation on fish in aquaculture facilities
(fish farms) and rivers. While the populations recovered over time
and the eastern and Asian stocks appear stable, the western stock
along the Aleutian Islands has fallen 70–80% since the 1970s. In
1997 the western stock of Steller sea lions was listed as endangered.

The California Sea Lion *(Zalophus californianus)* is a coastal
eared seal native to western North America. Its natural habitat
ranges from southeast Alaska to central Mexico, including the Gulf
of California. Extensive commercial killing of California sea lions
caused great losses in the populations. Although the species was
subsequently afforded some protection, sea lions continued to be
hunted until the latter half of the 20th century in certain areas of
California and Mexico for sport, pet food, hides and other uses.
Large numbers were also captured for display and entertainment
in zoos and aquariums. The species was placed under protection
in the United States in 1972 by the Marine Mammal Protection Act,
and the killing of California sea lions has been banned in Mexico
and Canada since 1969 and 1970, respectively. The estimated population today is more than 200,000 for the U.S. stock; 80,000 for the
Western Baja California stock; and 30,000 for the population in the
Gulf of California.

ELEPHANT SEALS

Northern elephant seals *(Mirounga angustirostris)* are a wide-ranging pelagic species that once lived throughout most of the eastern Pacific. Hundreds of thousands of northern elephant seals once thrived in these waters and had their rookeries on these coasts and islands. For most of the year they are far out at sea. They typically give birth and breed at their rookery December-March and return again later in the year for several weeks to molt. They can dive deep to find food and avoid white sharks, a major predator. Researchers have recorded elephant seal dives almost a mile deep and they have been recorded underwater for almost two hours thanks to some remarkable physiological adaptations.

Elephant seals were slaughtered wholesale from about 1818–1869 for the oil that could be rendered from their blubber, using the oil for lamps and lubrication. The meat and skins also sometimes had some value. The hunt was so intense that elephant seals were thought to be extinct by the end of the 1800s. A small group of eight seals was discovered on Guadalupe Island in the 1880s, but scientists killed seven to gain as much information as possible on this extinct species.

Fortunately, that was not all of them, and the population slowly recovered. In 1922, the Mexican government gave protected status to elephant seals, and the U.S. government followed suit a few years later. Slowly the population grew and spread. The first elephant seals on Año Nuevo Island in California were sighted in 1955, and the first pup was born there in 1961. In 1981 the first breeding pair was seen at Pt. Reyes and now more than 900 can be seen. The total population is now estimated to be close to 150,000.

OTHER FUR-BEARING ANIMALS

Native life and ecosystems on land and sea were disrupted in ways we can barely imagine. Removing a million foxes had to make a difference, as would taking out more than a half million wolves! The landscapes and ecosystems that scientists started to study in the 20th century had often been shaped by the catastrophic level of removals during the 1800s. Several species, like the Guadalupe Fur seal, probably lost much of their genetic diversity from passing through very tight genetic bottlenecks; as a result, they may now be at greater risk from disease outbreaks and environmental change.

Kelp

Giant kelp *(Macrocystis sp.)* forests are dominated by float-bearing plants up to 150 feet long that grow from the bottom and spread thick canopies across the sea surface. Giant kelp flourishes in wave-exposed areas with nutrient-rich cool water ranging from 20–120 feet deep. The kelp attaches to rocky areas on the sea floor with a holdfast. Reefs and rocks are preferred but giant kelp can also be found growing on sand with the holdfast on exposed worm tubes or the remains of old holdfasts. Giant kelp has provided resources for humans for thousands of years. They also support a rich complex community of animals, fish and invertebrates.

Giant kelp absorbs nutrients from the water through all its surfaces. Under optimal conditions fronds can grow up to two feet per day and a large kelp may have more than 100 fronds. Kelp forests produce as much oxygen by photosynthesis as the Amazon rainforests, with 100 times less biomass. Kelps can live for up to 25 years.

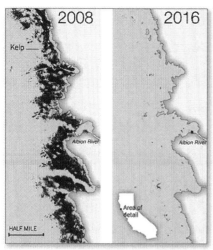

Kelp decline Northern California

In a recent study, California kelp only occupied a third of the range measured in 1911, and that was likely much less than originally found on the coast before the sea otters were wiped out in the 1820s and 1830s. Kelp decline continues to be widespread. Dr. Tom Mumford from the Washington Department of

Natural Resources reports that floating kelp beds have all but disappeared from southern Puget Sound. Declines are also reported generally from the Salish Sea, including the coast of British Columbia. The northern coast of Washington has done better, perhaps due to the return of sea otters.

Some fish graze on kelp and will damage kelp forests when present in large numbers. Sea otters helped control these fish. Invertebrates such as sea urchins, amphipods, isopods, and other species can also eat or damage kelp and were once eaten in great numbers by sea otters. Studies of otters near Pacific Grove showed they were eating more than 100 urchins a day. The removal of the sea otter from California and Baja California eliminated the key predator on sea urchins and other kelp eaters. The loss of otters and kelp make the sea coast ecosystem much less productive. A study in Alaska found that nearshore productivity was two to five times higher in areas with sea otters and kelp.

The many fish that eat urchins and other kelp-eaters have also been virtually eliminated in many areas by commercial and recreational fishing. Sea urchins ranked only 7th in relative importance in the diet of the long-lived California sheephead (*Semicossyphus pulcher*) at San Nicolas Island, but when the fish were removed from experimental areas the sea urchin population increased 26% in the first year. Each sheephead was eating more than twenty urchins a day, or about 8,000 urchins per hectare every year.

Archeological sites in the Channel Islands suggest the sheephead was both highly

Bull kelp decline Ocean Cove

abundant and an important target of fishing activities by native peoples.

Analysis of bones showed they were first in abundance at many sites. The average size of sheepheads along the northern Channel Islands today is significantly smaller than in the past as a result of commercial and recreational anglers and deteriorating ecosystem health.

OTHER RISKS

Changes in climate and pollution can trigger harmful algal blooms that kill large numbers of marine animals. Only a few species of algae are responsible for problems like paralytic shellfish poisoning (PSP). This results from a number of saxitoxin derivatives produced by dinoflagellates in the genus *Alexandrium*. In 1799, more than 150 Aleut sea otter hunters were poisoned and 100 died after eating contaminated mussels. An increase in PSP activity has been suggested in some southern California sites, most notably in commercial shellfish growing areas in Santa Barbara and San Diego counties. Domoic acid poisoning (DA) is caused by diatoms in the genus *Pseudo-nitzschia*. These can affect people who ingest the poisons in food. DA poisoning has also led to thousands of sick or dead seals, sea lions, sea otters, dolphins, birds, and whales along the west coast in recent years. DA has been detected in seafood species along the California coast (bivalve shellfish, sardines, anchovies) almost every year since 1991. After otters, other predators (including lobster) and fish are removed sea urchin populations can increase exponentially and overgraze the kelp, creating "urchin barrens." Once threshold urchin densities are attained, phase shifts between kelp beds and barrens are relatively abrupt. Destructive grazing creates positive feedback mechanisms that accelerate the shift to barrens. Actively grazing sea urchins have unlimited, high quality food, and that enables them to grow rapidly and reproduce quickly. In these urchin barrens the sea floor is dominated by the purple and red spines of urchins as they scour the rocks for food. Only the hard, calcified, pink crustose algae can withstand the high-impact urchin grazing. Recovery can be very slow as the urchin barrens are fairly stable. One diver compared the current depauperate kelp beds with a visit to a Serengeti Plain in Africa that no longer had any of the large mammals.

The decline of the kelp forest exhibits many of the problems facing restoration ecologists. You can't easily fix an ecosystem by considering just one part. A good kelp forest needs sheephead fish, sea

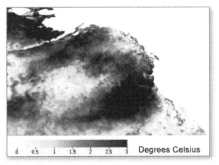

Degrees Celsius

Sea surface temperature anomaly September 2019.

otters, sea stars, crabs, clams, lobsters and more. Trying to restore just one part can be helpful but is likely to require persistent and costly efforts for success. The giant kelps are also becoming a victim of global warming as rising temperatures change wind patterns and reduce nutrient rich upwelling.

The ocean warming events of 2013–2016 and 2019 caused extensive damage to kelp. Abnormally high sea surface temperatures reduce the upwelling of nutrients that the giant kelp need to prosper. Warming temperatures are also damaging native villages as permafrost melts, storms ravage coastlines no longer protected with sea ice, and erosion nibbles and gobbles the shoreline. Many villages will need to be relocated and rebuilt. Outside support will be needed. Lifeways have also been altered as thin ice or no ice makes traditional hunting dangerous or impossible.

CHAPTER 5

Lessons Not Yet Learned

This book should make it clear that we have, can, and will ignore ecological and cultural damage in the pursuit of profits and power; but we do so at our peril. The Fur Trade in the West clearly demonstrates the damage caused by the failure to consider the cultural and ecological costs.[64] The Hudson's Bay Company fur brigades to California in 1832–33 are a good example. John Work and Michel Laframobise led their men (and women and children) south into California and spread deadly malaria.[65] The two leaders returned to Ft. Vancouver with a fair number of beaver pelts and made a modest profit.

The impact of the disease was clear even as they returned north in the fall of 1833, with many of the brigade still sick themselves. In his journal on August 6, 1833 Work noted, *"The villages that were so populous and swarming with inhabitants when we passed that way in Jany or Febry last seem now almost deserted & have a desolate appearance. The few wretched Indians who remain seem wretched they are lying apparently scarcely able to move."* As George Yount later recalled, *"The bodies of untold thousands lay whitening the plains and fertile valleys.... Deserted and desolated village sat tenantless all over the valleys..."* Jonathan Warner remembered, *"The banks of the Sacramento River, in its whole course through the valley, were studded with Indian Villages, the houses of which, in the spring, during the day time were red with the salmon the aborigines were curing... On our return, late in the summer of 1833, we found the valleys depopulated. From the head of the Sacramento to the great bend and slough of the San Joaquin, we did not see more than six or eight live Indians, while large numbers of their skulls*

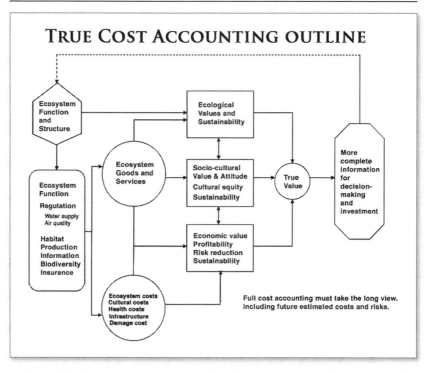

TRUE COST ACCOUNTING OUTLINE

and dead bodies were to be seen under almost every shade tree, near the water, where the uninhabited and deserted villages had been converted into graveyards." As many as 50,000 people may have died for 2,000 beaver worth about $4,000. This is less than 8¢ for everyone that died.

The ecological damage was equally catastrophic. Within thirty years of its discovery the Steller sea cow[66] was extinct. This remarkable beast would have been very valuable for humans in many areas of the world if it had not been wiped out. In less than 50 years the sea otter was extinct in many areas and would soon be gone throughout almost the entire original range. The populations of beaver, seals, sea lions and other species were severely affected by intense hunting efforts. In some cases, as with beaver, it was deliberate.[67] In most cases it was simply the open market of greed and ignorance.

Alexander Kashevarov, the *kreol* who became a ship captain, map maker and ultimately brigadier in the Russian Navy, clearly saw and described the ecological collapse of sea otters, fur seals, sea lions and other fur bearing animals. Before the fur trade, all of these animals had lived and multiplied while providing sustainable critical resources for the native people. Kashevarov argued that only the natives understood the animals well enough to manage them[68] and thus should be ceded control over Alaska's environment. William Sturgis also saw the value of the native cultures and recommended returning ownership of much of the coast back to the First Nations, *"the whole extent of the coast from Mendocino in latitude 40, to Prince William Sound, latitude 60, could be left in quiet possession of the native and rightful proprietors of the soil, it would be better for the civilized world, even in a political point of view, to say nothing of these moral considerations..."*

The destruction of so many native people resulted in further changes to the plant and animal communities as collecting, hunting, management with fire, and fishing declined or stopped.

TREAT YOUR PEOPLE WELL

The fur trade offers many good examples of the value of treating people with respect and rewarding workers. The positive example is Captain William Sturgis. His fair trading practices earned him many friends in the native communities and he never had to suffer or resort to violence; it was one of his proudest achievements. He was a capable commander who was well regarded by his crews and managed many successful round-the-world voyages.

Captain William Sturgis

As a ship owner he was careful with his budgets and expenses but tried hard to ensure good working conditions for the crews of his ships. Richard Henry Dana sailed on a Bryant and Sturgis ship and remarked on the care and consideration of this owner, who visited the ship before it sailed and told the sailors what to expect and what to bring with them. He rightly pointed out that the violence against fur ships on the northwest coast was commonly the result of cruel and often vicious treatment of the native communities by ship captains operating with greed, terror and violence.

Ill-treatment and lack of respect could lead to disaster. Captain Thorn of the *Tonquin* abused the local leader and got his crew killed and ship destroyed. In 1785, James Hanna, captain of the *Sea Otter*, abused the local chief. This contributed to the taking of the *Boston* and death of all but two of her crew in 1803. They were also incensed because the captain had abandoned hunters on the Farallon Islands and only a couple had successfully made the 900-mile trip home.

The mutiny on the *Llama* was also the direct result of ill-treatment of Kaigani sea otter hunters, compounded by the frustration of hunting in areas where the otters had almost been exterminated. On November 18, 1838, after two days of hunting at San Miguel Island, two kayaks came back to the ship with only three skins. Captain Bancroft verbally abused them and sent them back out to hunt again. On the 20th, two kayaks came in from Santa Rosa Island with only eight skins, and a little later, Mr. Robinson, the ship's mate and also a hunt leader, arrived with just four more. Bancroft was incensed and further enraged when Robinson reported that the hunters had been quarreling over the skins. When Bancroft signaled by gunfire for all kayaks to come back to the boat, none obeyed. Robinson then returned to the island with orders to hunt around it thoroughly before going to Santa Cruz Island. On the 23rd, Captain Bancroft saw kayaks coming from the direction of Santa Cruz Island and by 11am all were on board.

The captain began to insult them in their own language, so that the American crew could not understand what was being said. At last it appeared to be settled and the captain went down to dinner. When he came up on deck again the argument flared anew and the hunters passed their guns up from their kayaks. Captain Bancroft headed to the forecastle and after a tussle he ran aft and jumped up on the rail, saying something the American crew imagined might have been, *"Fire if you dare,"* for they immediately fired and he fell mortally wounded. At the sound of the shots the other three white men on board, a few kanakas (Hawaiians) in the crew, and the captain's wife jumped up from their dinners and rushed to the deck. Running to her husband, Mrs. Bancroft threw her body on his and begged for his life, but she was shot and wounded. One of the white crewmen named Graydon tried to reach his gun and was killed with a shot to the head.

The Kaiganis took possession of the ship and had the mate take them home. They reached home on December 26 and after stripping the ship of many of its effects and keeping most of the furs, they let the crew and ship go, leaving 5 skins and 21 tails as a present for Mr. Robinson for getting them home safely. The *Llama* arrived in Hawaii on January 13, 1839 and Mrs. Bancroft died two weeks later. No further action was taken against the Kaigani. They eventually sold the furs through the Hudson's Bay Company.

Cascading Ecosystem Impacts

The removal of the sea otter led to dramatic losses in kelp as the sea urchin populations exploded. The loss of kelp may have contributed to the extinction of Steller's sea cow. The loss of kelp also reduced productivity of entire ecosystems. This meant less fish, fewer invertebrates, and impoverished ecosystems with less food and fewer resource options for people.

The removal of the beaver triggered significant hydrologic changes and streams that once flowed in the summer dried up. Increased flood intensity as the beaver dams failed without maintenance led to channel cutting, erosion and cut bank formation in the more arid areas of the west. Changes in river flow and channel stability and wetlands also affected a wide range of plant, insect, animal, and bird species. Changes in the environment from overgrazing by elk and cows also worked against beaver recovery. When wolves were returned to Yellowstone they reduced elk grazing along streams and allowed plants to grow that in turn enabled the beaver to return. Beaver provide a range of benefits for water conservation, wildlife habitat, and recreational opportunities. As in so many other areas we would do well to return to the management practices of the First Nations.

Although the eco-sciences have made many strides in the last 100 years, there is still much we do not know. Most critically we don't know what the Fur Trade ecosystems in the west were like before they were damaged. We don't fully understand these systems today, often fail to recognize that they once were much different, and are even less sure of the long-term effects of pollution and rapid climate change for the future. We can be sure these will offer unwelcome surprises.

Wherever we look, more detailed research soon shows us how incomplete our knowledge is, even for things we are most familiar with. Yet even with what we do know we can make progress in protecting and restoring marine and riverine ecosystems, strengthening communities, and improving economies of rural ares.

"How little we know and how much there is to learn. Research and investigation along any given line show how incomplete is our knowledge even of the things with which we are most familiar. There is nothing new under the sun, but there is always something we do not understand about the subjects to which we have given the most thought and study."
—Marcus Petersen[69]

We need to learn more with field work. We need more research in environmental history. We also need to listen carefully to the tribal elders. The question we need to ask more forcefully is, "How does this action or project contribute to, or detract from, sustainability from a long-term ecological and cultural perspective?"

IMPROVING MANAGEMENT

We need to better understand what happened in the past in order to more accurately comprehend what we see today. This can enable us to develop better management strategies for a more sustainable future. Ecological restoration provides opportunities to better understand how these ecosystems function and can create mutually beneficial relationships between us and the non-human landscape. The old notion of wilderness must be replaced with an understanding that people and non-human entities have been dancing in a continuous co-evolution for 13,000 years in the Fur Lands of the West. If we pay attention and rethink the way we do business and live we can improve the quality of life for all. The function and structure of many ecosystems and social systems is not well understood because they are complicated with many cross-links and feedback loops. Changes may unfold slowly but inexorably or very quickly.

Funding for basic research has been declining in recent years, and field work has fallen out of favor because it is messy and takes too long. Fortunately, much of the research that is needed is not costly, requiring little more than time and expertise. Educating and supporting skilled volunteers can make a big impact. Developing funding that is consistent over many years is needed to support training for skilled para-botanists, para-ecologists, para-sociologists, and para-accountants; they can do high-level research under the supervision of experts. College, high school, and even middle school students can also provide meaningful research and restoration support.

As examples of this kind of approach we can look to the Hatfield Marine Science Center in Newport, Oregon with 40 years of research and an innovative path to the future with Oregon State University's Marine Studies Initiative. This will blend the natural and social sciences through innovative curriculum development and interdisciplinary research. The recently formed Ecosystem Restoration Camp efforts now underway have over 400 members from more than 30 countries. Projects are underway, but a Marine Restoration and Science Program is needed. This could include many of the features of the California Conservation Corps (CCC), which currently provides work and educational opportunities to about 1500 young adults and veterans each year at more than two dozen residential and nonresidential locations throughout the state. In 1976 Governor Jerry Brown signed today's CCC into law. He envisioned the program as "a combination seminary, kibbutz, and Marine Corps boot camp." B.T. Collins, the CCC's director from 1979–1981, coined the CCC's motto: "hard work, low pay, and miserable conditions." Participants get work experience and educational opportunities to complete their GEDs and continue onward. The budget in 2018 was $90 million with about half of the budget coming from work projects sponsored by various governmental and nongovernmental entities reimbursing the CCC for the work performed.

I would suggest a series of thirteen Marine Ecosystem Restoration and Science Corps programs from the Aleutians down to Cedros Island, Mexico. These camps would include education, training, and hands-on experience in marine research, ecosystem monitoring, marine restoration, history, archeology and cultural geography. Many would be co-located, cooperative projects with the First Nations.

For the interior areas hit hard by the removal of the beaver and wolf, I would suggest several Stream Restoration Camps to restore streams, protect riparian areas, re-establish beaver communities, and stabilize and improve stream flow for critical summer months. These corps members could also assist in emergencies, as the California Conservation Corp does.

PROPOSED MARINE ECOSYSTEM RESTORATION CAMPS

- Aleutian Islands, Unalaska, Alaska (Co-op Aleutian-Pribilof Center)
- Kodiak Island, Alaska (Co-op Kodiak College)
- Sitka, Alaska (Co-op University of Alaska, SE)

- Tahsis, BC (Co-op Captain Meares Elementary Secondary School)
- Skidegate, BC (Co-op UBC)
- Chinook, Washington (Co-op Portland State University)
- Makah, Washington (Makah Cultural and Research Center, Co-op Evergreen College)
- Newport, Oregon (OSU, add to existing program)
- Ft. Bragg, CA (Co-op Mendocino College)
- Santa Cruz, CA (Co-op UCSC)
- Goleta, CA (UCSB)
- Channel Islands (Catalina Island Marine Institute and CSU, Channel Islands)
- San Diego (Co-op SDSU)

PROPOSED STREAM RESTORATION CAMPS

- Bitterroot, Montana
- Winthrop, Washington
- Pit River, California

A better understanding of the ecosystem science is also needed and long-term interdisciplinary research projects are essential. The National Science Foundation's Long-Term Ecological Research sites are, unfortunately, almost unique. Today more than 2,000 researchers are involved at 28 LTER sites. These are woefully underfunded, with about $30 million each year spread over 26 sites. In 2019 the National Science Foundation (NSF) grants added funding for a Long-Term Ecological Research[70] (LTER) site in the northern Gulf of Alaska. This new LTER site was awarded $5.6 million over five years. The complex food webs in this region have been, and will continue to be, affected by human activities, short-term environmental variability, and long-term ecosystem and climate changes.

The Northern Gulf of Alaska LTER offers Research Experience for Teachers. This includes opportunities to participate in science activities while sailing with researchers on their periodic cruises.

These teachers actively participate in research activities and communicate the experience to their students and the general K-12 community via web-based logs (blogs) and videos. They also bring new insight and knowledge to their classrooms.

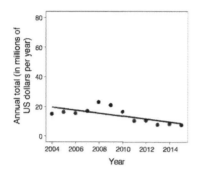

NSF Long Term Funding

Each site could easily use base funding of $5 million to $10 million a year, and there should be many more of them to cover a wider range of ecosystems, both natural and under restoration. This would cost only $90 million a year.[71] LTERs are needed for Puget Sound, the Columbia River, the Greater Yellowstone Ecosystem, the northern California Kelp Forest, and the Southern California Kelp Forest.

What Research is Needed?

A much better understanding of ecosystem structure (how things are organized) and function (how things work) is needed to develop more cost-effective, successful restoration projects and more sustainable resource management efforts. A broad range of research is necessary (sea otters to kelp, climate change and killer whale diet, wolves to beaver dams), and all should be related to past, current, and potential future behavior and use. The interaction between resource management and the economics and policy drivers must also be considered more carefully. The scale of research should extend from the microsite to the landscape as well as from the family to the community to the culture.

Research should be multidisciplinary and involve a range of scientists, engineers, economists, anthropologists, First Nations, psychologists, artists, designers, marketers, managers, and students who are working on common problems. Research on the successes and failures of existing ecological restoration projects is needed.

The benefits of restoration on biodiversity and ecosystem structure and function should be evaluated carefully. The importance of protecting cultural diversity to maintain biological diversity needs to be better understood as well.

A Long-Term Cultural Research program can be developed with the First Nations to help them respond to the many challenges they face from past ill-treatment. Research agendas for long-term cultural research sites would include the many problems that have proven intractable due to incomplete cost accounting and a lack of focus on sustainability. It is critical to understand the past in order to better manage the future.

More research on sustainability and true cost accounting is urgently needed. The fundamental change from business and government as we know them today—to how we must know them in the future—is the recognition that we must always consider environmental and social impacts in developing true cost accounting. The fur trade examples included in this book make this very clear. The focus must change from short-term profit (cash only) to long-term appreciation of economic, social and natural capital. This revolution will create many opportunities for research and for entrepreneurs who create businesses, services and products that enhance sustainability. The growing market for sustainable sea foods is a good example.

Sustainability is not simply about the environment, but also must include a healthy economy and programs, policies and traditions that provide support for community, safety, cohesion, cooperation, education, health and equity. This definition of sustainability is sometimes referred to as the triple bottom line (social, economic, environmental) or the 3Ps: People, Prosperity, Planet. One of the first steps toward this type of true cost accounting has been the effort to report and improve organization sustainability.[72] Growth in the number of sustainability reports has been quite rapid, with more than 10,000 now prepared annually worldwide. Examinations of resource management have also improved,[73] but sustainability reporting and true cost accounting remain in their formative stages, and funding is needed to support research and development of more accurate reports that lead to change.

   First and foremost, we need to pay attention. Aldo Leopold, a hunter, fisherman, land manager, scientist, and professor, learned by looking. His writing should be required reading for all high school and college students. As he came to realize...

> *A thing is right when it tends to preserve the integrity, stability, and beauty of the biotic community. It is wrong when it does otherwise.*
> —Aldo Leopold (1949)

WHAT YOU CAN DO

Get involved! Support your local or favorite group, place, and species with your time or money. Get out and help clean up, restore, and understand the marine environment, coasts, and rivers. Here

Restoration Class Scripps Knoll

are a few groups working for a healthier and more biodiverse West Coast—a more complete list is in the back of the book as Appendix 1.

- **Friends of the Sea Otter** works with state and federal agencies and other groups to maintain, increase and broaden the protection of the sea otter. Their goal is to educate the public about otters and to encourage action to recover this remarkable species.
- **Beavers Northwest** advocates for the many benefits of beavers through their research, outreach, and landowner assistance. An excellent resource.
- **The Beaver Institute** provides technical and financial assistance to public and private landowners experiencing beaver conflicts, supports scientific research, trains mitigation professionals, and increases public appreciation of the beaver's critical role in creating healthy wetland ecosystems.
- **Martinez Beavers** advocates for beavers in the Bay Area and provides education and information about the value of these wonderful animals.
- **The Society for Ecosystems Restoration** in Northern BC works to restore vulnerable and degraded ecosystems in northern British Columbia. Members include representatives from academia, government agencies, industry, First Nations, NGOs, non-profit and community-based organizations, local and regional experts, and other stakeholders. There is no cost to join the SERNbc.
- **The Society for Ecological Restoration Western Canada** includes British Columbia, Alberta, Saskatchewan, Manitoba, the Yukon, and the Northwest Territories.
- **SERCAL (The California Society for Ecological Restoration),** is a membership-based organization dedicated to advancing the science, art, and practice of restoring native California habitats.
- **The Society for Ecological Restoration** is a global community of restoration professionals that includes researchers, practitioners, decision-makers, and community leaders from Africa,

Asia, Australia/New Zealand, Europe, and the Americas. SER members are actively engaged in the ecologically sensitive repair and recovery of degraded ecosystems utilizing a broad array of experiences, knowledge sets, and cultural perspectives.

- **The Mid-Vancouver Island Habitat Enhancement Society** is dedicated to the recovery of wild Pacific salmon through the conservation and restoration of their habitat—watersheds, estuaries and shorelines. It works to connect people to their landscape through partnerships that focus on field study, education and restoration.
- **Adopt-A-Stream Foundation** encourages Pacific Northwest communities to protect and enhance the watersheds on which they live. Members are invited to participate in regular events with great networking and community-building potential.
- **The American Cetacean Society (ACS)** is a non-profit, volunteer membership organization headquartered in San Pedro, California with 7 regional chapters in the U.S. The Puget Sound Chapter works for the protection of marine mammals.
- **The Center for Whale Research** is a membership organization for people, companies and organizations who support the study and preservation of resident Orcas in Puget Sound.
- **Puget Soundkeeper** is a founding member of the Waterkeeper Alliance. They monitor Puget Sound water quality, help set strong policies and regulations that protect our waterways and our health, enforce environmental regulations, engage citizens and businesses in waterway cleanups and recovery projects, educate and involve the public in local water pollution issues, and partner with local and regional groups to advance solutions that protect Puget Sound.
- **The Oregon Coast Alliance** works with coastal residents to protect and restore coastal and marine natural resources; educate the public and decision makers, advocate sustainable land use, and are involved with the adaptation to climate change.

- **Get Inspired**'s programs are designed to inspire stewardship and curiosity for the natural world through the exploration of science in schools. Projects include kelp and abalone restoration work. Truly inspiring!
- **The Pacific Marine Mammal Center** rescues, rehabilitates, and releases marine mammals, and inspires ocean stewardship through research, education and collaboration.
- **The Bay Foundation** works with a broad group of stakeholders, including government agencies, environmental groups, local communities, industry and scientists, to create and put into action innovative policies and projects that clean up waterways, create green spaces in urban areas, and restore natural habitats. Work includes preserving wetlands, kelp forests, and abalone in Santa Monica Bay.
- **Save The Bay** works to restore San Francisco Bay by protecting and restoring San Francisco Bay for people and wildlife, uniting the Bay Area to create a clean and healthy environment. As climate change and pollution threaten the bay, they lead initiatives to make the region sustainable for future generations.

CLIMATE CHANGE

- **350.org** works to build a global grassroots climate movement that can hold our leaders accountable to the realities of science and the principles of justice. That movement is rising from the bottom up, all over the world, and is uniting to create the solutions that will ensure a better future for all. Their online campaigns, grassroots organizing, and mass public actions bring together a global network active in over 188 countries
- **Friends of the Earth** and their network of grassroots groups in 77 countries fight to create a healthier, just world. Their current campaigns focus on clean energy and solutions to global warming, protecting people from toxic and potentially harmful technologies, and promoting smarter low-pollution transportation alternatives.

University and college programs can increase your understanding and ability to help protect and restore the Fur War coast and rivers.

Take a class, earn a certificate or pursue an AA, BS, MS or PhD. Here are few to consider (more included in Appendix 2).

- **British Columbia Institute of Technology** offers BS and MS in Ecological Restoration. Learn to be an ecosystem physician and help heal our degraded ecosystems.
- **University of Victoria, British Columbia**—BS/BA, MS/MA in Restoration of Natural Systems.
- **The Coastal Research Institute** was established as a program of the Frank R. Seaver College of Science and Engineering at Loyola Marymount University and The Bay Foundation. The goal is to engage LMU faculty, undergraduate and graduate students in multidisciplinary, hands-on approaches to research related to coastal resource management and restoration in Los Angeles.
- **The Gulf of California Marine Program at Scripps Institution of Oceanography at the University of California San Diego** is a team of scientists, students, and professionals from multiple disciplines and institutions who are dedicated to generating and disseminating scientific information that has a direct, positive impact on conservation and resource management issues in the Gulf of California region, Mexico.
- **Simon Fraser**—Canada's first master's program in Ecological Restoration is offered as a joint program between the British Columbia Institute of Technology and Simon Fraser University.
- **University of British Columbia, Vancouver**—one class, UFOR 403 Ecological Restoration, Ecological principles relevant to restoration of ecosystems.
- **University of Alaska, Southeast**—Alaska Native Languages and Studies examines three primary components of modern and historical Alaska Native life: language, art, and society. Taught by Alaska Native professors.
- **University of California, Davis**—The UC Davis Graduate Group in Ecology is the largest and most comprehensive ecology

graduate training group of its kind. They also offer a BS in Ecological Management & Restoration.

- **UC Santa Barbara**—The Cheadle Center for Biodiversity and Ecological Restoration, satisfies the university's obligation to provide good stewardship of campus lands. The Center encourages land restoration on and near campus and has a facility dedicated to education, research, and outreach related to regional biological diversity and restoration.

- **University of Alaska, Anchorage**—The Department of Geography and Environmental Studies offers a BS in Environment & Society and minor in Environmental Studies. The Environment and Natural Resources Institute is an interdisciplinary group of core staff and faculty affiliates with the shared goal of improving understanding of environmental and natural resource issues in cold regions. Also available an Alaska Native Studies Minor.

PRIVATE COMPANIES

Much of the restoration research and education is done by companies working in these fields. Training is applied and often more specific and detailed than university work. The River Design Group is one example.

Dam removal Rogue River: the River Design Group provides meaningful careers for engineers, biologists, hydrologists, surveyors, ecologists and fluvial geomorphologists.

Acknowledgments

First, my thanks to the journal keepers and diarists, the people who preserved these records and the diligent librarians who have digitized so many original sources. Google Earth has been very helpful in understanding the relations between historical events, trading posts, and fur trails.

Thanks also to the information aggregators, H. H. Bancroft, H. M. Chittendon, Canadian biography, Wikis from several countries, encyclopedias, fur trade blogs and web page developers, and others. I am also most appreciative of the expedition artists who did such amazing work under often difficult conditions. Louis Choris, John Webber, James Madison Alden, Paul Kane and Alfred Jacob Miller were especially helpful.

And finally, I also would express my appreciation for the writers who have led the way: Harold L. Innis, Stephen R. Brown, James R. Gibson, Richard Somerset Mackie, Ilya Vinkovetsky, Lydia T. Black, Lynn H. Gamble, Mary Malloy, and so many others. As the great environmental historian George Perkins Marsh said, *"I shall steal pretty much, but I do know somethings myself."*

I have been fortunate to visit many of the fur outposts, to paddle on the Columbia headwaters and British Columbia lakes and rivers up to Ft. St. James; to visit, hike and paddle in Alaska and to hike and camp in the Rockies, Sierras, San Juans and other mountains and deserts of North America. I have always been interested in ecology, ecological restoration and environmental history, and this book enabled me to bring these all together.

Thanks also to family, colleagues, and friends who contributed to my understanding of ecosystems and ecological restoration. Many have also supplied support, encouragement, information, editing and a variety of images and documents for this book that I might have otherwise never seen.

I would also like to thank Sutton Mason for her editorial assistance, and David Wogahn for book design.

David A. Bainbridge
San Diego, 2020

Further Reading

1. ## GEOPOLITICS
   - Giraldez, A., J. Sobredo, D. O. Flynn, eds. 2017 [2002]. *Studies in Pacific History: Economics, Politics and Migration.* CRC Press.
   - Gutiérrez, R. and R.J. Orsi, eds. 1998. *Contested Eden: California before the Gold Rush.* UC Press.

2. ## ECONOMICS
   - Mackie, R. 1997. *Trading Beyond the Mountains.* University of British Columbia Press.
   - Gibson, J. 1992. *Otter Skins, Boston Ships, and China Goods.* McGill-Queens University Press. (exceptional)
   - Dolin, J. 2010. *Fur, Fortune and Empire.* W.W. Norton.
   - Black, L.T. 2004. *Russians in Alaska.* University of Alaska Press. (exceptional)

3. ## CULTURE
   - Anderson, M. K. 2013. *Tending the Wild.* UC Press. (exceptional)
   - Gamble, L. H. 2008. *The Chumash World at European Contact.* UC Press. (exceptional)
   - Langdon, S. 2013. *Native People of Alaska, Traditional Living in a Northern Land.* 5th Ed. Greatland Graphics.
   - Williams, Maria Sháa Tláa, Editor. 2009. *The Alaska Native Reader: History, Culture, Politics.* The World Readers.
   - Muckle, R. J. 2014. *First Nations of British Columbia.* UBC Press.

- Heizer, R. F. and M. A. Whipple. 1972. *The California Indians: A Source Book.* UC Press.
- Powers, S. 1976 [1877]. *Tribes of California.* UC Press.
- Lewis, A.B. 2016 [1907]. *Tribes of the Columbia Valley and the coast of Washington and Oregon.* (now also on Kindle)

4. ECOLOGY

SEA OTTER

- Nickerson, R. 1984 *Sea Otters: A Natural History and Guide.* Chronicle Books.
- Palumbi, S. R and C. Sotka. 2011.*The Death and Life of Monterey Bay.* Island Press.
- Braje, T.J. and T.C. Rick, eds. 2011. *Human Impacts on Seals, Sea Lions, and Sea Otters: Integrating Archaeology and Ecology in the Northeast Pacific.* University of California Press.
- Ogden, A. 1941. *The California Sea Otter Trade: 1784–1884.* University of California Press.

BEAVER

- Ryden, H. 1989. *Lily Pond: Four Years with a Family of Beavers.* William Morrow. (exceptional)
- Lanman, C.W., K. Lundquist, H. Perryman, J. Eli Asarian, B. Dolman, R. B. Lanman and M. Pollock. 2013. *The historical range of beaver (Castor canadensis) in coastal California and the San Francisco Bay Area: An updated review of the evidence.* California Fish and Game 99(4): 193–221. (exceptional)
- Lanman, R. B., H. Perryman, B. Dolman and C. D. James. 2012. *The historical range of beaver in the Sierra Nevada: a review of the evidence.* California Fish and Game 98:65–80.
- Gibson, P. P. and J. D. Olden. 2014. *Ecology, management, and conservation implications of North American beaver (Castor canadensis) in dryland streams.* Aquatic Conservation and Management of Freshwater Ecosystems 24: 391–409.

- Ripple, W. J. and R. L. Beschta. 2012. *Trophic cascades in Yellowstone: The first 15 years after wolf reintroduction.* Biological Conservation. 145(1): 205–213.
- Pollock, M. M., G. M. Lewallen, K. Woodruff, C. E. Jordan and J. M. Castro, Eds. 2017. *The Beaver Restoration Guidebook: Working with Beaver to Restore Streams, Wetlands, and Floodplains.* Version 2.0. United States Fish and Wildlife Service, Portland, Oregon. 219 pp. Online at: https://www.fws.gov/ oregonfwo/promo.cfm?id=177175812

Fur Seals and Sea Lions
- Kirkwood, R. and S. Goldsworthy. 2013. *Fur Seals and Sea Lions.* CSIRO Publishing.
- Gentry, R. L. 2014. *Behavior and Ecology of the Northern Fur Seal.* Princeton University Press.

Kelp
- Druehl, L. and B. Clarkston. 2016. *Pacific Seaweeds: Updated and Expanded Edition.* Harbour Publishing.
- Kopczak C.D., D. Navarro, and D.E. Navarro. 2006. *The California Kelp Forest: Science & Activity Guide for Teachers.* Manta Publications. https:// dornsife.usc.edu/assets/ sites/291/ docs/ SC_KELP_BOOKsm2.pdf
- Foster, M. S. D. C. Reed, M. H. Carr, P. K. Dayton, D. P. Malone, J. S. Pearse, and L. RogersBennett. 2013. *Kelp Forests in California.* in Research and Discoveries: The Revolution of Science through Scuba. Smithsonian Contributions to the Marine Sciences. 39:115–132.

5. Lessons

- Bainbridge, D. A. 2006. *Adding ecological considerations to "environmental" accounting.* Bulletin of the Ecological Society of America. October. 8(4):335–340.
- Bainbridge, D.A. 2020. *True Cost Accounting.* www.truecostalways.com.

- Cone, M. 2000. *Mystery: Why is the Aleutian ecosystem collapsing?* Worldcatch News Nov 7, Center for Biological Diversity. https:// www.biologicaldiversity.org/species/ birds/ spectacled_eider/ worldcatch.html
- Kurlansky, M. 2020. *Salmon.* Patagonia Books.
- Leopold, A. 1949. *A Sand County Almanac: And Sketches Here and There.* Oxford University Press. (exceptional)
- Elkington, J. 1999. *Cannibals with Forks the Triple Bottom Line of 21st Century Business.* Capstone, Oxford.
- Barg, S. and D. Swanson. 2004. *Full Cost Accounting for Agriculture.* International Institute for Sustainable Development. Winnipeg.

Appendix 1
MORE GROUPS THAT WORK ON PROTECTION AND RESTORATION OF THE AREAS AFFECTED BY THE FUR WAR

The Mattole Restoration Council is one of the oldest community-led watershed restoration organizations. Established in 1983, the Council's primary mission is to understand, restore and conserve the ecosystems of the Mattole River watershed, with attention to threatened Coho and Chinook salmon and steelhead.

The Beaver Advocacy Committee of the South Umpqua Rural Community Partnership (SURCP) supports restoring viable beaver populations with the purpose of establishing wetlands to enhance Coho salmon and aquatic species populations.

The Occidental Arts & Ecology Center (OAEC) is a research, demonstration, education, advocacy and community organizing center in West Sonoma County, California. It develops strategies for regional scale community resilience and the restoration of biological and cultural diversity. They support a Bring Back the Beaver Campaign to educate citizens about the importance of beaver.

Watershed Guardians is a community-based organization focused on helping make the natural world around us a better, happier place. Work on restoring watersheds with beaver reintroduction and support.

The Mid Klamath Watershed Council has been actively planning, coordinating and implementing restoration projects in the Mid

Klamath sub-basin for almost 20 years. They focus on projects that directly benefit our anadromous fisheries resources. They work with volunteers to implement practical, hands-on restoration projects while educating participants on restoration techniques and stewardship principles.

Elkhorn Slough Foundation's mission is to conserve and restore Elkhorn Slough and its watershed. They see Elkhorn Slough and its watershed protected forever—a working landscape, where people, farming, industry, and nature thrive together as one of California's last great coastal wetlands. With counts exceeding 100 animals, Elkhorn Slough has the highest concentrations of sea otters on the California coast.

Columbia Riverkeeper's mission is to protect and restore the water quality of the Columbia River and all life connected to it, from the headwaters to the Pacific Ocean.

Scientists of the Northwest Fisheries Science Center conduct leading-edge research and analyses that provide the foundation for management decisions to protect, recover, restore, and sustain ecosystems and living marine resources in the Pacific Northwest. They carry out important work on beaver dams for stream restoration. An excellent resource.

Oregon Wild supporters work to protect and restore our wildlands, wildlife, and waters as an enduring legacy for future generations. They have a video series on Oregon Wildcast: The Lost Sea Otters of Oregon. I highly recommended this.

The Alaska Sealife Center is the only public aquarium and ocean wildlife rescue center in Alaska.

The Alaska Climate Adaptation Science Center provides managers with the tools and information they need to develop and execute management strategies that address the impacts of climate change on natural and cultural resources. Hosted by UAF with a USGS hosted office in Anchorage, AK.

The Alaska Wildlife Alliance advocates for healthy ecosystems, wildlife, and habitat in Alaska. Working to reform wildlife public policy, they focus on predator control, hunting and trapping regulations, marine mammal issues, impacts of commercial use of wildlife, development impacts, public participation in wildlife policy, and public education regarding Alaskan wildlife.

The Nature Conservancy uses science to help safeguard Alaska's lands and waters for nature and people. They protect and restore salmon habitat in Bristol Bay, Matanuska-Susitna Basin, and in the Tongass.

The Alaska Wilderness League works to protect Alaska's most significant wild lands from oil and gas drilling, and from other industrial threats. Starting in 2004, AWL expanded its work to include ecologically significant areas of Alaska's vast National Petroleum Reserve, the Tongass National Forest, and the outer continental shelf areas of the Beaufort and Chukchi Seas.

The Kachemak Bay Conservation Society is concerned with environmental protection of the Kachemak Bay and Kenai Peninsula region.

The Northern Alaska Environment Center (AEC) has been working to protect some of the wildest country left in North America since 1971. The vast Interior and Arctic regions of Alaska include 293,000 square miles of largely pristine wilderness, 3,200 miles of coastline, and incalculable miles of streams and rivers.

The Southeast Alaska Conservation Council is a coalition of 15 groups in Southeastern Alaska working to maintain the health of the Tongass National Forest—the largest remaining temperate rainforest on Earth.

The Wildlife Federation of Alaska is dedicated to conserving Alaska's fish, wildlife, and habitat for the benefit of present and future generations. WFA involves and educates people in decisions affecting habitat conservation and promotes the stewardship and enjoyment of Alaska's fish and wildlife resources. Members are involved in habitat conservation to ensure that future generations will be able to enjoy Alaska's fish and wildlife.

The Forest Ethics Solutions Society is located in Vancouver and is focused on the continued implementation of the Great Bear Rainforest and Canadian Boreal Forest Agreements. It also protects endangered forests, wild places, wildlife, human wellbeing, and our climate from the threats posed by logging and the pursuit of extreme oil such as tar sands. They have helped secure the protection of more than 65 million acres of forest.

Water First supports efforts to improve water resources and fish habitat for indigenous people. Their fish habitat restoration work focuses on rebuilding and improving fish spawning grounds of local fish species that have been damaged due to human activity or eroded over time. By improving spawning sites, this habitat restoration work aims to improve fish populations for future generations. Community members participate in the assessment, planning and restoration phases of a fish habitat restoration project, in partnership with experts in biology and hydrology. Elder consultations are key to identifying historically active fish habitat and restoration sites. Local youth are hired and receive training to implement the project with expert guidance.

Ecojustice goes to court and uses the power of the law to defend nature, combat climate change, and fight for a healthy environment for all. Their strategic, innovative public interest lawsuits lead to legal precedents that deliver lasting solutions to our most urgent environmental problems.

Center for Environmental Policy & Law is the only "water watch-dog" advocacy organization dedicated exclusively to protecting Washington rivers and streams.

Wild Steelhead Coalition is a volunteer driven advocacy group dedicated to increasing the return of wild steelhead to the waters and rivers of the Pacific Northwest. All who care about this threatened species are welcome.

American Cetacean Society—Puget Sound Chapter members and supporters work for the protection of marine mammals like whales and porpoises. Regular events provide relationship building, volunteer, and networking opportunities.

Center for Whale Research is a membership organization for people, companies, and organizations who want to support the study and preservation of resident Orca whales in the Puget Sound.

Conservation Northwest has helped protect hundreds of thousands of acres of wildlands, supported the recovery of threatened species from wolves to fishers, and touched thousands of lives throughout the greater Northwest. Elected leaders, government agencies, and conservationists know them for being science-based and tenacious, yet pragmatic.

Long Live the Kings (Salmon) programs support saving wild salmon and steelhead trout from extinction in their home waters. Attending an event, volunteering, and donating are great ways to get involved.

The Marine Conservation Institute is dedicated to securing permanent, strong protection for the oceans' most important places—for us and future generations. The Marine Conservation Institute uses the latest science to identify important marine ecosystems and advocate for their protection.

The Washington Environmental Council People for Puget Sound program is dedicated to protecting and restoring the sound to health. Puget Sound is the largest estuary in the country by volume, rich with ecological diversity. The region is also the lifeblood for urban and rural communities that rely on the sound for economic opportunity and a high quality of life.

Forterra acquires and preserves critical farm, wild, and urban land for community use and future generations in the Puget Sound region. Attend an event or volunteer!

The Friends of the San Juans was established in 1979 to help preserve the beauty, character, and wildness of the islands in the face of increasing development. Friends' primary goals are to foster wild and healthy shorelines, promote thriving and sustainable communities, conserve forests, farmlands, freshwater and prairie habitats, and ensure the health of the marine ecosystem. Friends uses science to make informed decisions that conserve the county's environment and economy.

Washington Wild is a movement to protect wild places, starts from the ground up—bringing together activists, community leaders, tribes, elected officials, farms, faith leaders, businesses, agencies and organizations all in the name of conservation. Washington Wild and its supporters have played an instrumental role in permanently protecting nearly 3 million acres of designated wilderness throughout Washington State.

Skagit County established the Skagit County Marine Resources Committee as part of the congressionally authorized Northwest Straits Marine Conservation Initiative. Their stated purpose is to act as a catalyst for the protection and restoration of the marine waters, habitats and species of Skagit County to achieve ecosystem health and sustainable resource use.

Los Angeles Waterkeeper works on kelp forest restoration.

The Watermen's Association connects sportsmen to map out areas for small groups to clear sea urchins. They ask individuals to self-report their efforts.

The Ocean Protection Council was created to help ensure that California maintains and restores a healthy, resilient, and productive ocean and coastal ecosystems for the benefit of current and future generations. The Council was created pursuant to the California Ocean Protection Act signed into law by Governor Arnold Schwarzenegger.

Reef Check trains thousands of citizen scientist divers who volunteer to survey the health of coral reefs around the world, and rocky reef ecosystems along the entire coast of California. The results are used to improve the management of these critically important natural resources. Reef Check programs provide ecologically sound and economically sustainable solutions to save reefs by creating partnerships among community volunteers, government agencies, businesses, universities and other nonprofits.

The Noyo Center for Marine Science grew out of public and municipal efforts to diversify and revitalize the economy and community of Fort Bragg at the former Georgia-Pacific Mill Site as redevelopment began. Through workshops and meetings, the Fort Bragg community identified a marine science and education center as a high priority to anchor the initial Mill Site recovery and help generate living wage jobs in the community.

The Northwest Environmental Advocates holds its own in negotiations, spearheading strong environmental positions. NWEA's actions are supported by science, law and policy, tempered by an understanding of practical considerations. NWEA uses the full range of techniques — from litigation and negotiation to education and organizing.

Citizens for a Healthy Bay has brought people together to achieve a clean and healthy Commencement Bay and the surrounding eco-system that calls Puget Sound home. Their work is driven by a passion for the natural environment and our community.

Puget Sound Restoration Fund works collaboratively to restore marine habitat, water quality, and native species in Puget Sound through on-the-ground projects. They are committed to a vision of a clean and healthy sound that is productive, full of life, and one that sustains us.

The Hood Canal Environmental Council is an organization of people who cherish Hood Canal as a unique spot in Puget Sound with its unusual marine, mountain, and forest scenery, its many relatively pristine watersheds, and its clean marine water.

The Friends of Grays Harbor is a broad-based citizen's group made up of crabbers, fishers, oyster growers and caring citizens. They work to foster and promote the economic, biological, and social uniqueness of a healthy Grays Harbor estuary.

WaterWatch protects and restores water to Oregon's rivers, streams, and lakes for fish, wildlife, and people. They speak for the public interest. to help pass balanced water legislation and, when necessary, go to court. Their goal is to ensure a legacy of healthy rivers in Oregon.

Rogue Riverkeeper works to protect and restore clean water and fish populations in the Rogue River Basin through advocacy, accountability, and community engagement.

Umpqua Watersheds envisions a land of lush mountains and river valleys which sustain an abundance of clean water, diverse wildlife, and native fish runs. These landscapes will enrich a community that values fulfilling jobs, diverse viewpoints, and the solitude of wild places.

The Friends of Willapa National Wildlife Refuge provides support for the Willapa National Wildlife Refuge. Specific projects requiring Friends' attention include trail maintenance, habitat restoration, threatened and endangered species inventory and monitoring projects. The Friends helped restore streams providing ten miles of spawning and rearing habitat and 149 acres of estuary.

The Monterey Bay National Marine Sanctuary is a federally protected marine area offshore of California's central coast. with a shoreline length of 276 miles and 6,094 square statute miles of ocean, extending an average distance of 30 miles from shore. It is larger than Yellowstone National Park.

The Greater Farallones National Marine Sanctuary includes the area 3,295 square miles north and west of San Francisco Bay. The GFNMS Advisory Council helps guide management and outreach.

The Greater Farallones Association conserves the wildlife and habitats of the sanctuary through scientific research, environmental education, and community-based conservation. Following the Sanctuary Advisory Council's recommendations, they have created a comprehensive Bull Kelp Recovery Plan for the Greater Farallones National Marine Sanctuary.

Orange County Coastkeeper is one member of a larger coalition of partners in Southern California working to restore populations of abalone throughout Baja (Mexico) and Southern California.

The Ballona Wetlands Land Trust is dedicated to the acquisition, restoration, and preservation of the entire Ballona Wetlands ecosystem in Los Angeles.

The Batiquitos Lagoon Foundation is dedicated to the preservation, enhancement, and protection of Batiquitos Lagoon, one of the few remaining tidal wetlands on the southern California coast. The BLF is also involved in programs to educate the public in the values of this natural environment (coastal salt marsh with tidal mudflats) and the habitats it provides for birds, insects, plants, fish, mammals, and benthic animals.

Friends of the Dunes is dedicated to conserving the natural diversity of coastal environments in Humboldt County, California, through community supported education and stewardship programs.

Golden Gate Audubon Society works to understand, educate, and restore the Bay Area environment for birds and other creatures. GGAS is the lead for wetlands restoration at Martin Luther King Jr. Shoreline in Oakland and Pier 94 in San Francisco. They organize monthly volunteer habitat restoration events at a total of eight sites operated by five different public agencies on both sides of the Bay. GGAS advocacy has helped launch restoration projects at the Emeryville Crescent, Berkeley Meadow, Eastshore State Park, Heron's Head Park, Alameda Wildlife Reserve, Crissy Field Lagoon, Yerba Buena Island, and Pier 94.

Los Angeles Audubon Society protects birds and their habitats, speaking out against legislation that threatens these based on scientific evidence. They also advocate for conservation strategies that will preserve natural open space and encourage bird and wildlife-friendly designs of the urban built environment. LAAS has played a key role in Snowy Plover and Least Tern Conservation.

Mendocino Coast Audubon Society is dedicated to providing exciting learning opportunities for students, adults, and families who are interested in becoming more knowledgeable about the birds and conservation issues on California's North Coast. MCAS works on conservation with breeding surveys, monitoring, and habitat restoration.

The Monterey Audubon Society is dedicated to conserving and celebrating the birds and wildlife of the greater Monterey Bay region. They engage in an array of educational, citizen-science, and advocacy initiatives geared toward protecting the region's birds and its biological diversity.

The Monterey Bay Aquarium's Conservation & Science programs tackle some of the most critical issues affecting ocean health. They bring decades of expertise and relationships in ocean science, policy and markets to the task of restoring kelp forests, marine mammals and ocean ecosystems.

The Northcoast Environmental Center promotes understanding of the relations between people and the biosphere and to conserve, protect, and celebrate terrestrial, aquatic, and marine ecosystems of northern California and southern Oregon.

The Redwood Region Audubon Society promotes wise, balanced, responsible, and ethical use of natural systems on a local, national, and global scale; and protects the biotic and abiotic components of local, national, and global natural systems.

The Nature Collective works to preserve and restore San Diegan lands, including the San Elijo Lagoon. Their mission is to create a passion for nature, for all. We want our places and events to offer every human an experience and a deep connection with the living world.

The Morro Coast Audubon Society promotes protection for birds, endangered species, critical habitats, important ecosystems, and the scientific management and protection of wildlife.

Nimiipuu Protecting the Environment is committed to protecting Tribal Treaty rights within their original ceded area and usual and accustomed places. They work to protect and carry on time-honored sustainable environmental practices in the tradition of the Nimiipuu. Their vision is that the Nimiipuu and community members live, work, play, and pray, in an environment which sustains such activities and leaves a healthy environment for future generations.

The Wild Olympics Campaign is a coalition working to protect wild forest and river watersheds on the Olympic Peninsula. These watersheds provide local communities with clean water, world class outdoor recreation opportunities and sustain the outstanding Peninsula way of life. They are vital to the health of Hood Canal and Puget Sound and are critical habitat for wildlife, steelhead, and salmon.

The mission of the **Willapa Hills Audubon Society** is to support ecologically responsible ways of life, to help maintain biologically diverse habitats, and to promote environmental understanding and enjoyment of nature.

The Friends of the Elephant Seal is a non-profit organization dedicated to educating people about elephant seals and other marine life and teaching stewardship for the ocean off the central coast of California.

Sociedad de Historia Natural Niparajá is a La Paz-based NGO whose mission is "to perpetuate the natural assets that distinguish Baja California Sur, as a result of actions by consensus and with scientific basis, for the benefit of local communities, and present and future generations."

The Mexican Fund for the Conservation of Nature is a non-governmental, not-for-profit organization and the first environmental endowment fund in Mexico. MFCN's mission is to financially support and strengthen efforts for the conservation and sustainable use of biodiversity in Mexico.

Pronatura Noroeste is the regional chapter of the National Pronatura System, Mexico's longest standing and largest conservation organization. Pronatura Noroeste operates in the northwestern part of the country, where economic activities depend greatly on natural resources. It runs seven environmental programs including one on marine conservation and sustainable fishing.

Comunidad y Biodiversidad (COBI)—COBI is a non-profit organization dedicated to promoting the conservation of marine biodiversity in coastal communities of Mexico through community participation.

The Nature Conservancy works to conserve the lands and waters on which all life depends. They have initiatives underway on the Baja Peninsula, including San Quintin Bay.

World Wildlife Fund works to ensure that the Gulf of California remains a healthy and productive marine area that can support local communities as well as the abundant wildlife within and near its waters. They have helped create several protected areas within the Gulf and have worked to protect areas such as Cabo Pulmo National Marine Park from any future coastal development.

The White Abalone Restoration Consortium is made up of many groups, all working toward expanding scientific knowledge of white abalone and increasing public awareness of the first marine invertebrate listed as endangered in the United States. The WARC is working to restore the species.

Appendix 2
ADDITIONAL ACADEMIC AND TRAINING PROGRAMS TO LEARN MORE ABOUT THE FUR COAST AND HELP WITH CULTURAL AND ECOLOGICAL RESTORATION

Washington State University— Environmental and Ecosystem Science BS covers interactions of physical, chemical, and biological conditions of natural and human-modified environments, with the goal of solving growing environmental challenges. Wildlife Ecology & Conservation Sciences includes wildlife research and teaching facilities with grizzly bears, deer, bighorn sheep, endangered rabbits, and amphibians.

University of Washington—ESRM students can minor in ecological restoration. The Master of Environmental Horticulture degree is a coursework-based, professional degree that focuses on restoration, horticulture, and environmental management. Undergraduate and graduate students from all disciplines may earn the Restoration Ecology Certificate. The UW-Restoration Ecology Network is a tri-campus program, serving as a regional center to integrate student, faculty and community interests in ecological restoration and conservation. UW Bothell offers a minor in ecological restoration.

Western Washington University—MS in Biology, Marine and Estuarine Science.

Colorado State University—Restoration Ecology Major, online degree Master of Natural Resource Stewardship.

The Colorado Forest Restoration Institute is a science-based outreach and engagement organization hosted by the Department of Forest and Rangeland Stewardship and the Warner College of Natural Resources at Colorado State University.

University of Arizona—BS, MS, PhD in Ecology, Management, and Restoration of Rangelands.

Humboldt State—Environmental Science & Management degree offers a major or minor in Ecological Restoration.

San Jose State — BS Environmental Science with a Concentration in Environmental Restoration and Resource Management

Western Colorado University—MS Environmental Management, interdisciplinary training for building environmental and community resilience.

University of Idaho—Restoration Ecology Undergraduate and Graduate Academic Certificates.

Montana State University—BS and MS offering in Land Rehabilitation.

New Mexico State—Offers an interdisciplinary, undergraduate program in Conservation Ecology.

University of Montana, Missoula—BS in Ecosystem Science and Restoration.

University of Nevada, Las Vegas—The Abella Lab conducts restoration ecology and applied conservation science research informing conservation and management, often in direct collaboration with resource managers and other scientists. Their key areas of expertise include plant, forest, desert, fire, and restoration ecology.

University of Nevada, Reno—Ecological restoration courses included in several degree programs, e.g. the Master of Science in Natural Resources and Environmental Science.

University of Utah—Land Management, Conservation and Place emphasizes how management techniques such as mitigation, restoration, and planning are informed by ecological, cultural, and social understandings.

Utah State University—Offers courses that are open to everyone wishing to learn more about aquatic ecosystem restoration. Workshops for Continuing Education Units. USU graduate students can earn credit toward the Post-baccalaureate Certificate in Aquatic Ecosystem Restoration.

University of Wyoming—The Wyoming Reclamation and Restoration Center helps to maintain and protect Wyoming's land, air, water and wildlife by promoting restoration of the complex components and functions of disturbed ecosystems.

University of Lethbridge, Alberta— Offers a 2-year diploma in Environmental Assessment and Restoration.

UC Berkeley—Offers a Conservation and Resource Studies major.

UC Irvine—The Masters in Conservation and Restoration Science is offered through the Department of Ecology and Evolutionary Biology and the Center for Environmental Biology.

UC Merced—The Environmental Graduate Group focuses on understanding the earth as an integrated system that includes the atmosphere, hydrosphere, lithosphere, and biosphere.

Cal Poly San Luis Obispo—Land Rehabilitation and Restoration Ecology Minor.

Cal Poly Pomona—The multidisciplinary Master of Science degree in Regenerative Studies prepares individuals for active professional and research roles aimed at finding successful solutions to environmental problems in the 21st century.

Saddleback Community College— Offers an ecological restoration certificate.

American River College—Offers an AS degree in Environmental Conservation, an interdisciplinary program that advances the understanding of ecological systems and their interrelationships, including those with human society. Field methods and study design, and conservation and management of ecosystems.

Merritt College—Environmental Management and Restoration Technology program prepares students for employment in the fields of environmental restoration and management.

Lewis and Clark College—Restoration Ecology AAS degree, Restoration Ecology Certificate of Proficiency.

Evergreen College offers programs in Human Communities and the Environment, Natural History and Environmental Sciences.

Portland Community College— Environmental Studies, Biology and Landscape Technology students have an extremely diverse living laboratory to observe and study within the campus boundaries.

University of Northern Arizona—Offers several degrees in forestry and one in fire management, as well as a Forest Health and Ecological Restoration Certificate. The Ecological Restoration Institute is nationally recognized for mobilizing the unique assets of a university to help solve the problem of unnaturally severe wildfire and degraded forest health throughout the American West.

Montana Tech—Is currently considering a proposal for a MS in Ecological Restoration (available soon). Students can customize their studies to fit their career goals and objectives. It will be available to students enrolled on campus and to working professionals seeking professional advancement via distance learning.

Many other schools and colleges may offer related programs, certificates, classes, or workshops. Extension programs and workshops can be very rewarding.

Illustration Credits

COVER
- Mark Myers

TITLE PAGE
- Burning Opitsaht DB

PRELUDE
- 1.1 Baidarkas Henry Wood Elliott
- 1.2 Baydar welcome William Smythe
- 1.3 Salish village Spanish expedition artist
- 1.4 East bay tribes map DB

1. GEOPOLITICS
- 1.1 Shitik DB
- 1.2 Promyshlenniki head DB
- 1.3 Iliuliuk Gavril Sarychev
- 1.4 Sitka Yuri Lisyanski
- 1.5 Russia fur routes DB
- 1.6 Fort Ross A. B. Duhaut-Cilly
- 1.7 Cook's ships John Webber
- 1.8 Astoria Gabriel Franchère
- 1.9 Ft San Miguel Sigismund Bacstrom
- 1.10 Geopolitics DB
- 1.11 Oregon City John Mix Stanley

2. ECONOMICS ILLUSTRATIONS
- 2.1 Storm Russian artist adapted by DB
- 2.2 Golden round DB
- 2.3 Sea otter raft DB
- 2.4 Ships NW DB
- 2.5 Otter prices DB
- 2.6 Otters to Canton DB
- 2.7 Baidarka storm DB

Look for volume 2

Tenacity

Remarkable people of the Fur War
1765-1840

David A. Bainbridge

More resources, illustrations lesson plans and maps at:
https://www.furwar.com/supplemental-material
https://www.furwar.com/blog

Notes

The Challenge of History

1. Considered by many as one of the greatest of all time, directed by Akira Kurosawa 1950
2. More properly the Seliñ or Salish
3. Washington Irving's "Astoria" (1836) is a good example

Prelude

4. Often called the Pompeii of mud, digging deeper they found ruins of another buried village from a slide 850 years ago.

Chapter 1

5. I found more than 100 epidemics on the fur coast from 1765–1840
6. Nakba in Arabic: النکبة, al-Nakbah "disaster", "catastrophe", or "cataclysm"
7. Kayaks with 1, 2, or 3 cockpits, sometimes incorrectly called canoes. The standard fur trade model had three cockpits; two for men and one for the catch or for a Russian passenger. They could travel 10 miles per hour.
8. One native critic has called this period, "Auschwitz with roses"
9. Some cruises were made in open boats similar to the Viking long ships, but most were often crude one-or two-masted decked vessels built in Kamchatka or Okhotsk that gave more protection for the crews. Later schooners, brigs and other larger sailing ships were used.
10. Or a bit earlier
11. In Sitka and other outposts, the Russian men married and lived with Tlingit and other native women, and by 1840 the mixed race *kreols* made up almost half the population of Sitka. These individuals could go to Russia for education but had to work for the RAC for many years in return.
12. A rather unusual agreement between a nation and a company
13. The native people more likely considered it a lease
14. Often rounded up by crimps (thugs) who sold them to the ships
15. It had already been rebuilt once—Redivivia in Latin. Ships could wear out quickly if not well maintained or run on to too many reefs or sand bars.
16. Some consider this a case of mercantile capitalism but there is a growing recognition that it might better be called war capitalism. It was so profitable because it was done with greed, theft, subjugation, slavery and violence.

CHAPTER 2

17. To avoid taxes and regulations and ease entry to port
18. Even today, modern fishing ships with skilled crews, sophisticated instruments, and maps are too often lost.
19. The RAC, HBC and NWC company flags are all based on the national flag.
20. Humans may have only 2,000 per square inch
21. About 5 rubles per dollar (comparing costs and exchange rates is fraught with difficulty)
22. The Russians referred to mixed race people, typically a Russian father and native mother, as *kreols*.
23. By other comparisons of value difference then and now this could be $125 million
24. Values varied widely from place to place and month to month, but my best guess is the value of goods here was about 70 skins, so the ship made out quite well.
25. In 1733 Father Sigismundo Traval had seen sea otters on Cedros Island in such numbers that they killed some with sticks and sent them to Mexico City.
26. Treated with a dilute solution of mercury salts dissolved in nitric acid. Steaming would then release the mercury in vapor, poisoning the workers, hence the phrase "mad as a hatter."
27. Trading post
28. The central and highland plateau area of what is now British Columbia
29. Workers were sent to this cold, wet, dangerous and dreadful outpost (lacking fresh water) as punishment.
30. As an aphrodisiac in the Asian markets
31. About 10 pounds each or about 15,000 walruses
32. Export numbers here were not broken out by District but many were from the West Coast or western mountains
33. The value of a shilling varied but was often about 22¢
34. The fishing falls also known as Celilo Falls or *Wy-am*

CHAPTER 3

35. Nakba Arabic: النكبة, al-Nakbah "disaster", "catastrophe", or "cataclysm"
36. For a more detailed exploration, focusing on the eastern coast see William Cronon's excellent book, "Changes in the Land: Indians, Colonists, and the Ecology of New England".
37. Often called Aleut
38. Some suggest it is more likely the first epidemic diseases came in the 1500s.
39. Perhaps triggered by a landslide or earthquake
40. The Grande Ronde reservation in Oregon includes fragments of more than 30 tribes. Some chiefs were reported to speak more than 10 languages.
41. The Russians applied the name Aleut (probably a Siberian name) to all the native people of the Aleutians, Kodiak Island, and other parts of the Alaska Peninsula. Sugpiaq is a popular self-designator on the Kenai Peninsula today,

while Alutiiq is more common in the south and Kodiak archipelago. This makes unravelling history challenging as it is often unclear who is being discussed.

42. Unangax, Unangan (singular), sometimes used interchangeably with Aleut.
43. Alutiiq
44. Often called Koniag
45. Artels
46. People of the Tides, Kaloshes, Klinket, Chilcoots, Chilcats, Koloshes, etc.
47. Their fort proved impenetrable but an accident cost them most of their gunpowder and they could not continue to fight. If they had been able to fight longer they may well have killed Baranov and changed the fate of Alaska natives.
48. Today Nuu-chah-nulth is preferred, but in older literature also Nutka, Aht, Nuuchahnulth, Tahkaht. Other Nootka tribes included: Ahousaht, Chaicclesaht, Clayoquot, Ehatisaht, Ekoolthaht, Hachaath, Hesquiat, Kelsemaht, Klahosaht, Kwoneatshatka, Kyuquot, Manosaht, Muchalat, Nitinat, Nuchatlitz, Oiaht, Opitchesaht, Seshart, Toquart, Uchucklesit, and Ucluelet. Closely related Makah, Ditidaht and Pacheedaht (many different spellings).
49. On a private mission but an officer of the British Navy.
50. Comcomly recognized the mate of the *Albatross* when he returned after sixteen years and also remembered the name of the ship's captain.
51. Also known as *chinuk wawa*
52. An oral tradition from the Clatsop told of a shipwreck and the introduction of a spotted disease about 1780.
53. Also known as the Interior Salish
54. To touch the enemy was considered the greatest honor because it was riskier and took more courage than shooting the enemy from afar.
55. In 1535, Cortez noted *"distressing deaths from . . . disease"* in the La Paz colony along the Pacific Coast of Mexico.
56. Sixteen epidemics (smallpox, measles, dysentery, and possibly influenza) were reported in northwestern New Spain from 1697–1770.
57. This may have been for trading with the other island people and coast.
58. There was enough water to later support 2,000–15,000 sheep
59. He was a young man and ill-equipped to manage the Koniag hunters. One letter suggests the order had been to move the islanders off to a more useful place for the RAC—perhaps Ft. Ross.
60. For more on Babin see his bio in Volume 2
61. Birds and feathers were used to make clothing in parts of Canada, Alaska, and Siberia.
62. The last native student boarding schools in Canada were not closed until the 1990s. In 2017 the Prime Minister of Canada, Justin Trudeau, apologized for the tragic effect the schools had on native culture.

CHAPTER 4

63. Large skin on frame boats

CHAPTER 5

64. Sometimes called full cost with consideration of internal and external costs of health, satisfaction, environmental decline, declining resource value, economic inequality
65. The intermittent fever; for more, see https://works.bepress.com/david_a_bainbridge/40/
66. *Hydrodamalis gigas,* related to the manatee and dugong but much larger
67. The Hudson Bay Company's attempt to create a fur desert.
68. The First Nations are becoming much more involved in managing the salmon for the same reason.
69. The Fur Traders and Fur Bearing Animals, 1914.
70. Despite the need, NSF long-term research funding has been on the decline. Hughes, B. B., R. Beas-Luna, A. K. Barner, et al. 2017. Long-Term studies contribute disproportionately to ecology and policy. BioScience. 67(3):271–281.
71. This is about the same cost as a single F35 fighter. The newest aircraft carrier costs a staggering $12.8 billion.
72. See for example the Global Reporting Initiative, https://www.globalreporting.org/standards/
73. Costanza, R. et al. 1999. Ecological economics and sustainable governance of the oceans. Ecological Economics 31:171–187. and Sipos, Y. 2005. True(r) cost accounting in agroforestry systems: An Introduction to the British Columbia Sustainable Agroforestry Calculator. Association for Temperate Agroforestry 2005 Conference Proceedings. 1–11. https://woodlot.bc.ca/atlas/wp-content/uploads/sites/2/2014/01/Sipos.pdf

Made in the USA
Columbia, SC
16 October 2020